Dedicated to the memory of
George Mure, Jill's husband and
Richard's friend who died
on July 9, 2003.

"We are absolutely outraged that
you have buggered off George,
just when we needed you
– we hope you approve".

BRUNY ISLAND – food from the edge of the world

Food and text by Jill Mure

Photography Richard Bennett

Published and distributed by Richard Bennett and Jill Mure

Richard Bennett
139 Matthew Flinders Drive, Alonnah 7150 Bruny Island, Tasmania
Telephone: 61 3 62931400 Mobile: 0418 120 209
email: richard@richardbennett.com.au
www.richardbennett.com.au

Jill Mure
Victoria Dock, Hobart, 7000, Tasmania
Telephone: 61 3 6229 6629 Mobile: 0407 873 116
email: jill@mures.com.au
www.mures.com.au

First published in Australia 2012 by Richard Bennett and Jill Mure
Reprinted by Everbest 2013

Graphics by de Vos design

Printing and binding by Everbest Printing Co Ltd in China

ISBN 978-0-9578110 6-5

BRUNY ISLAND
food from the edge of the world

Jill Mure

Richard Bennett

Kettering – gateway to Bruny Island

FOREWORD

Just eight months before the mutiny on the *Bounty*, William Bligh planted seven apple trees on Bruny Island. It was August 21, 1788. Although the little crop was soon ravaged by bush fire, one tree remained standing sound and proud as a portent for the future.

William Bligh would never know what he'd started!

The pages of this glorious book transport you through the colours, smells, sights and sounds of this raw and beautiful island as it is today.

It takes you to the extraordinary community of Bruny's boutique food producers. You will marvel at the unique epicurean range available and the enterprise and energy of these people who have chosen the island as their home.

Richard Bennett's superb images bring it all to life as they capture the quintessential quality and wild romanticism of this wonder that is Bruny.

He is blessed with a photo artist's fine skill to harness the light, form, allure and relevance of a subject with some playful whimsy thrown in. Richard has had a long love affair with the island and it shows.

Jill Mure's story weaving of the lifestyle and the seemingly endless offer of the finest produce, is a delight. Her recipes tell their own story as they were prepared with the locals who shared the finished dishes. When she told me this I was reminded of the cult movie "Babette's Feast", but this was pure Mure.

Her vast knowledge of food and its wonderfully varied applications put her among the elite of Australia's published foodies.

Is it too big a boast to claim there is nowhere else on the globe like this little patch of fecund earth, a skipping stone's throw from its 'mainland' Tasmania?

You have to go there to find the truth but this book begins the adventure.

The bountiful collection of photographs, stories and recipes squeeze the juice from the joy of living on Bruny Island. It's served with deep breaths of salty air carrying aromas of hot breads, rich cheeses, briny oysters and delicate wines. You can hear the grunt of fat black pigs, the sweet tweet of flame breasted robins and the swoosh of a mini bomber squadron of blue wrens casting flashes of shadow as they fly over verdant hills and sweeps of sandy bays.

Enjoy. Bon Appétit.

Judy Tierney

A LETTER FROM FRANCE

Everything starts inside a diplomat's comfortable living-room, opposite the Eiffel Tower, in the heart of Paris.

The Australian ambassador in France welcomes us in a gentlemanly manner. Aged about fifty, he was born in another island, smaller and less famous as its giant cousin Tasmania. He often returns there, and has never really left what he considers to be the most beautiful island of his country.

I am sitting in a sofa the size of the room, therefore quite unusual, and, opened on my lap, is a superb book of photographies, lent by my host.

As a producer, I intend to make a 52-minute documentary on Tasmania, for a series called 'Vu sur terre'. These films have been broadcasted every summer for the last 3 years, on France 5, a French channel.

Having learnt about the ambassador's Tasmanian origins, the whole production team has organized a meeting. The film has to portray Tasmanians in love with wild spaces.

Gradually I wander into the contemplation of the photographs. Each one of them is an invitation to travel and a silent promise of wonderful discoveries. Travellers know this: preparations before departures taste of anticipation and adventures to come. This book tells about a solitary and proud island, dotted with wild moors, huge lakes and rugged mountains.

Startling lights, breath-taking mountain heights, immense and deserted beaches, bold angles... All the photographs are inspired by the wilderness of Tasmania

Richard Bennett (and Bruny Island) had just burst into 'Vu sur terre' and into my life.

About a dozen mails and phone calls later, here we are, my cameraman and I, on the road to Bruny. On the road is not quite the right expression. Since Bruny is an island, you have to watch for the ferry, put the car on deck... and wait for the crossing time to pass. This is the instant of the ultimate eagerness, of the wind tingling your face, of the sun dazzling you. It is also the moment of the first looks, those you exchange just before you fall in love. They hold the end of expectation, the feeling of emotions to come. Bruny, whose coasts we are contemplating longingly, seems marvelously peaceful, almost indolent, as if the island was gently lolling around in this morning light of January.

It is so with exceptional places. They involve a lot of work, strength, energy and sometimes even exhaustion. Occasionally, they result in a struggle between the path leading to them and man travelling on that path. Exceptional places have to be deserved. They restore the balance between beauty and mediocrity.

Thus, it is a double satisfaction. You don't simply get the better of nature and its many obstacles, you also get the better of yourself.

Landing on Bruny is like arriving at the land of the Wizard of Oz. The enclosure of forgotten sensations. Those sensations of childhood, of sea spray tickling your nose, of long and deserted beaches, of the echo of waves losing itself in the fields of ripe wheat, of grey, deep blue or emerald waters, of wallabies looking at you questioningly before skipping away, of this fragile sand corridor linking the south with the north of the island, of those discreet houses hidden among eucalyptus, of these glistening lights appearing between clouds, of silent forests and dizzying cliffs.

Bruny is multi faceted, never quite the same, never quite different.

Bruny inebriates your senses. Everything is a question of instant. You will live these instants too as you peruse the following pages. This book is an eulogy on the beauty of a solar and radiant island.

Maud de Bohan

Nebraska Beach boat shed

CONTENTS

INTRODUCTION

We are living on an island, under an island, under an island, at the edge of the world. An old Bruny Island saying.

Tasmania is an island underneath Australia – and underneath Tasmania, there is a much smaller land mass called Bruny Island.

In 1642 the European explorer, Abel Tasman, was blown into the area before a gale. He then blew out again without making land fall, and suitably named Storm Bay on his way. He didn't realise that these were in fact islands. He called the entire land mass Van Diemen's Land, New Holland.

Tobias Furneaux was the next European explorer to sail into Storm Bay in 1773 in his ship Adventure. He'd set out from England as a support vessel to James Cook's Resolution on the second Voyage of Discovery. Lost in fog, James Cook went on to rendezvous in New Zealand, but Furneaux decided to first shelter in Adventure Bay and make repairs to his ship. He charted the bay, naming Penguin Island, Quiet Corner, Wooding Point and Watering Place. Watering Place was later named Resolution Creek after Cook's ship. And of course, the bay was named after his own vessel Adventure.

It was by pure serendipity that in 1792 Bruny D'Entrecasteaux discovered that the most southerly part of the Great Southland was an island. He had been searching for Lapéruse, the French explorer, who had mysteriously disappeared with his two ships somewhere in the Pacific, some two years before.

Bruny had injured his foot in rough weather and had handed over the helm of his sailing vessel the Recherche to his Sailing Officer Lieutenant Willaumez. They were making for the safe haven at Adventure Bay on the East Coast of the land mass. Erroneously, the ship was taken on a north-west bearing instead of due north. D'Entrecasteaux rose from his sick bed and was surprised by the quiet, calm waters – and where was Penguin Island? A sensitive, well educated man, he wrote in his journal that this part of the world felt like "a place quite separated from the rest of the universe". They had arrived in what is now known as Recherche Bay.

He sent his lieutenant, Saint Aignan to search for Adventure Bay. Aignan explored much further into "the channel" and waded across the shallow waters of what we now call Isthmus Bay. He found the neck, and in walking across this narrow strip of land realised that he had in fact stumbled upon Adventure Bay. He was the first European to cross the Isthmus. The Recherche then continued the exploration right up to the most northerly part of the channel and discovered that this indeed was an island. It was later named Bruny Island, in honour of this great French adventurer.

It wasn't until 1798 that Matthew Flinders circumnavigated Tasmania and declared it to be an island.

By the end of the eighteenth century Adventure Bay had become a popular destination for European explorers because of its constant supply of fresh water and good timber for ship repairs. These seafarers so far away from 'civilisation', met an indigenous, nomadic people, the Nuenonne, living contentedly on the island. They showed no fear of the white men in their strange clothes and peaceful exchanges were made. Gifts of beads, food and medals were given to the Nuenonne who, in return, gave crayfish, oysters and abalone to the visitors. These happy, smiling, peaceful, naive people were destined for a rapid decline, many of them dying from diseases, against which they had no immunity.

The whalers, who came in to the area in the early eighteen hundreds, were partly responsible for the complete decimation of these hapless people. For 40 years whaling was extremely lucrative and started a migration of European settlers to the island. Businesses were up and running with the felling of giant trees. Saw pits were opened, then a coal mine was started at Coal Point, this was followed by a soap and salt factory at Roberts Point. By the late nineteenth century Bruny Island was a thriving community with over 600 people working and living there.

This waterway was by then called the "D'Entrecasteaux Channel". It was a hive of industry with ketches and river steamers calling in at the 40 odd wharves and wooden jetties between Southport and Dennes Point. It was a highway to Hobart and the very lifeline for thousands of people wresting a living from this developing part of Tasmania.

The first commercial ferry was for the use of passengers only and started in 1938, plying between Tinderbox and Dennes Point. It wasn't until 1954 that Bruny Island acquired its first vehicular ferry *Melba*, which ran between Kettering and Barnes Bay. Things were looking good, until suddenly, in the early seventies, the population plummeted to just under 300 people.

This sudden decline was due to the collapse of important island industries. Established saw mills were closing; there was no longer a market for apples from the Apple Isle, as Tasmania was then called, when England joined the European Common Market; the IXL Jam Factory closed down; and the very lucrative Channel scallop industry collapsed due to the use of 'sputnik' dredges.

However, the wheel turns and there has, in recent years, been a mini population explosion on Bruny Island. People from all over Australia, in search of a new and more relaxed lifestyle, are buying land, building houses or renovating old family shacks. There has been an influx of people who care about the land and enjoy working in a fresh, clean and inspirational environment. They live and work surrounded by the most beautiful coastal scenery suffused with light and space.

Now the four and a half nautical mile crossing in the *Mirambeena* is made in less than 15 minutes. It seems to be just long enough to get the feeling that you are travelling 'off shore'. This holiday atmosphere is infectious and you find yourself happily chatting to complete strangers, as you queue for the ferry at Kettering. The wait for the ferry is made more comfortable by the eateries at either terminal. There is excellent coffee and David Roberts, the young cook at the Roberts Point terminal cafe, produces fabulous pies, soups and snacks using island produce.

There are over two hundred kilometres of touring roads on the island, some sealed and some gravel. North and South Bruny seem like two islands, but they are tied together by a narrow isthmus called "The Neck", which has the calm Channel abutting it on one side and Adventure Bay, with its often pounding surf on the other. This is where the fairy penguins can be seen at night coming ashore to nest and breed. The Channel is a favourite fishing and boating area because of its relative calm, but a plethora of fish are to be caught all round the island. Wildlife abounds and the birds of the island are spectacular. The drive from Dennes Point in the north, to the old Cape Bruny Lighthouse in the south, changes from sweeping white beaches, through green farmland, to densely wooded mountain slopes. The island's beauty is breathtaking. Standing on the wind torn cliffs looking south, one really is at the edge of the world.

This book is a collage of illustrated stories about a new wave of food producers, who have chosen to live on Bruny Island. There are the commercial producers some of them small and boutique. Others may produce simply enough for the family, but they all have one thing in common; it is their passion for the island and their produce.

CHERRIES

"When size matters". *Jon Grunseth*

This dazzling photograph was first used at Fruit Logistica in Berlin in 2009 to arouse awareness of a new Tasmanian cherry about to hit the world fruit market. It was the start of an exciting new export market for the Black Devil Tasmanian Cherry. It was the most heavenly large, sweet and very black cherry. Delivered all the way from Bruny Island, Tasmania, this cherry was destined to delight cherry-deprived customers in the depths of the European, Canadian and American winters. It was an instant success and in Paris and Amsterdam a two kilogram box of perfect cherries could fetch between €75 and €80.

I asked the engaging oversized Viking, Jon Grunseth, who started the cherry farm, why Tasmania and why cherries? – "Well, I absolutely loved Tasmania – just loved it; and hell, nobody has anything against cherries".

After retiring from the business world in 1997, Jon bought Lennonville at Alexander Bay on Bruny Island. It was a classic Tasmanian sheep farm with a spectacular homestead built by Major George Lennon in 1830. Jon, a wannabe agrarian, had to decide what to grow on this rugged strip of coastal land that had had sheep grazing on it for over a hundred years. After a great deal of research a vineyard was ruled out of contention because of a predicted worldwide wine glut. Essential oils and several other Tasmanian agricultural projects were considered but didn't seem to be quite the right answer. Cherries on the other hand, ticked all the boxes and so a new cherry farm was created.

There are now nearly 16,000 cherry trees in production, with origins as far afield as Canada to Czechoslovakia. The trees are all enclosed in huge netted canopies, which must have been a huge amount of work and an immense outlay. Pruning the trees efficiently and thinning the young cherries in early summer produce the largest cherries, which command a premium price. For example, a 30 millimetre cherry is nearly twice the value of a 25 millimetre cherry. So size really does matter.

Harvesting starts just before Christmas and finishes around Australia Day – a short but very sweet season – and they are not all shipped off the island. There is a small roadside stall at the Bruny Island Ferry Terminal, which sells kilo and half-kilo bags of the Black Devils. This treat will give you great pleasure on your island tour. They really are the best cherries you will have ever tasted and take it from me – you never buy enough.

Jon's recipe for cherries is to eat them directly from the tree after being chilled to 2°C.

PICKLED CHERRIES

Jill's Recipe – pickled cherries to go with pork rillettes, game, cold meats and pâtés.

500 ml red wine vinegar

350g Demerara sugar

3 cloves garlic, sliced

1 red chilli, thinly sliced

Zest of one orange

2 bay leaves

4 star anise

1 teaspoon cloves

1 tablespoon black peppercorns

500g cherries

Wash fruit and pack into sterilized jars. Bring all other ingredients slowly to the boil and pour over the cherries, making sure they are covered. Put lids on the jars. Keep in a cool dark place for three weeks before using. This pickle goes well with game, cold meats and pates served on Peter Barefoot's very easy bread recipe.

PETER BAREFOOT'S VERY EASY BREAD RECIPE

Peter is a gardening acquaintance whose garden is superb as is his bread recipe. The recipe yields two moist, satisfying loaves. He suggests freezing one for later in the week, which gives more time for the garden.

1 kg flour (strong) I sometimes use whole grain bread mix or other flours

2 heaped teaspoons dry yeast

2 tablespoons salt

1 litre cold water

Before going to bed, dry mix the flour yeast and salt. Stir in one litre of cold water. Cover with plastic and put in a cold place or the fridge overnight. In the morning, decant into two 500 gram loaf tins. Put into a cold oven. Put the oven temperature to 220°C. and bake for 45 minutes or until cooked. Sounds hollow when turned out and tapped on the bottom.

LAMB

"The mountain sheep are sweeter,
But the valley sheep are fatter;
We therefore deemed it meeter
To carry off the latter". *Anon*

Murrayfield Farm occupies nearly half of North Bruny. It stretches from Barnes and Great Bays on the West coast to Trumpeter and Variety Bays in the East. Five minutes after driving from the ferry along the B66 one is aware that the road is bordered by well kept fences and lush, green pasture. Sheep and lambs abound and there is definitely a sense of bucolic harmony in the air.

Murrayfield is outstanding as a well run sheep station of 4,000 ha carrying 15,000 Merino sheep. It is supported by all the modern technology that is available to today's primary producer, but Murrayfield has a past. The place names on the map give testament to the modern history of this land. Missionary Bay, Church Hill, St. Peter's Ruins and Robertson's Hills tell the story of the first pioneers who lived on the island.

But before the procession of 18th century explorers arrived on this land it was inhabited by a group of about seventy gentle and resourceful aboriginal people, the Nuenonne of Lunawanna-alonna, their name for Bruny Island. Endless fresh water and a copious supply of oysters, abalone, mussels, scallops and fish gave them an enviable seafood diet. Wallabies, seals, possums, seabirds, seeds, berries and roots were additional foods for these hunter-gatherers who wandered Bruny Island for many thousands of years. They sometimes crossed the Channel to visit their Tasmanian mainland relations in well constructed bark and string canoes.

In the early 19th century British settlers took control of Tasmania causing an inevitable clash with the Aboriginal people. European farming and whaling practices encroached on local hunting areas and sacred sites and by 1834 the last of the Nuenonne people were removed from Bruny Island.

The Davis family were the first settlers to build a house and start farming this land in 1824. Then others arrived. Eventually there was a group of small holdings covering the footsteps of the Nuenonne. During the 20th century the land was consolidated into one huge, successful property and the first-class Murrayfield wool crop became known as Murrayfield Gold. In 2001, because of its Aboriginal heritage, the sheep station Murrayfield was purchased by the Indigenous Land Corporation and became Australia's first 'indigenous-owned' commercial sheep station.

In 2001 Bruce Michael came to manage this culturally rich property. He was born into a South Australian sheep farming family and has background in (and an absolute passion for) Merino sheep, which is just as well, as he has 15,000 of these fine creatures to look after. Bruce's position is enviable and yet he has probably one of the most sensitive farming jobs there is.

Apart from normal, everyday farming practices, Bruce, his wife Lynne and son Todd, are conservators of the known thousands of indigenous artefacts that are scattered across these pastures. The land is sacred to the Nuenonne and as such must always be treated with the utmost respect. At the same time the biodiversity must be very carefully managed as Murrayfield is home to such endangered bird species as the white-bellied sea eagle, the forty-spotted pardalote, the Swift parrot and the wedge-tailed eagle. The Michael family also host young indigenous people who come to live on the farm whilst studying rural resource management. There are fantastic opportunities to learn about shearing, landscaping, revegetation and the fencing of artefact sites.

Bruce Michael is a legend and, with the backup of his family, is still able to follow his Merino passion to its utmost. The majority of the wool clip is sent to Patagonia where the wool is used in the manufacture of wet suits. The finest of Murrayfield wool is used in Japan for tailors who care. The pasture-fattened lambs are highly sought after at the indigenous butcher at Kingston Town. Customers like to know where their food comes from and that it has been well treated on the way.

I asked Bruce why Murrayfield lamb was so good and he assured me that it was because of the salt in their diet. This land is surrounded by sea and the sheep dine daily on saltbush. Then, as an afterthought, he added that "people who use Murrayfield lamb do so because they like to know where it comes from, but the most important thing is that they are very good cooks". On behalf of all those who cook Murrayfield lamb – I thank you Bruce.

Bruce's choice of cooking lamb is leg of lamb roast, just like Mum does. We all have a favourite recipe for roast lamb, be it with garlic or rosemary, slow cooked or flashed in a very hot oven and bleeding inside, served with mint sauce, redcurrant or medlar jelly. When Bruce came to dinner with us I gave him roast Kashmiri lamb, a recipe that I have been cooking for my family for years. He asked for the recipe so I think he liked it.

MURRAYFIELD LAMB KASHMIRI STYLE WITH CUCUMBER RAITA

2.5 kg leg of lamb

5 cloves garlic, crushed

1 tablespoon fresh ginger, grated finely

3 teaspoons salt

1 teaspoon ground cumin

1 teaspoon ground turmeric

½ teaspoon ground black pepper

½ teaspoon ground cinnamon

½ teaspoon ground cardamom

1 teaspoon chilli powder

¼ teaspoon ground cloves

2 tablespoons lemon juice

¾ cup plain yogurt

2 tablespoons macadamia nuts

1 teaspoon saffron strands

2 tablespoons honey

Remove the skin and excess fat from the lamb with a sharp kitchen knife then cut deep criss-cross slits all over it. Mix the garlic, ginger, salt, ground spices and lemon and add a little oil if the mixture is too dry. Rub the mixture over the lamb, taking care to push into the slits. Put yoghurt, macadamia nuts and saffron powder into blender and blend together until smooth. Spoon the puree over the lamb and then drizzle the honey over. Cover the lamb with foil and allow it to marinate overnight in the refrigerator.

Preheat oven to very hot, 230°C. Roast lamb in a covered baking dish for 30 minutes. Then reduce heat to a moderate 170°C. and cook for a further one and a half hours. Uncover lamb and allow to rest for 20 minutes before serving with hot rice and cucumber raita.

CUCUMBER RAITA

Lebanese cucumber, grated

4 tablespoons plain yoghurt

Grated rind of one lemon

Salt and pepper

Grate cucumber and drain on a paper towel. Leave for half an hour to soak up moisture. Add to the other ingredients and serve with the lamb.

MOROCCAN LAMB TAGINE

Jill's recipe – this Moroccan lamb tagine reminds me of a very special holiday in Morocco with Richard and Sue where we cooked and photographed and ate a very special tagine in Fez.

1 tablespoon olive oil

2 tablespoons whole blanched almonds

2 tablespoons pistachios, shelled

2 red onions, peeled

6 cloves of garlic, peeled

2 tablespoons grated ginger

Large pinch saffron threads

1 tablespoon coriander seeds, crushed

2 cinnamon quills

600g cubed lamb

400 ml hot water

6 dried apricots

12 prunes, pitted

Zest of 1 orange

2 tablespoons honey

Fresh coriander

Heat the olive oil in a large heavy-based casserole or tagine and brown the almonds and pistachios; remove and keep to add later. Sauté the onions and garlic until light brown then add the ginger, saffron, coriander seeds and cinnamon quills. Add the cubed lamb and stir until it is coated in the spices. Pour over the water and bring to the boil. Reduce to a simmer and cook covered either on top of the stove or in a medium oven. Test meat for tenderness after one hour. Add the apricots, prunes, honey and orange zest and simmer for a further half an hour. Taste for seasoning and stir in a handful of chopped coriander and the almonds and pistachios. Serve with coriander leaves scattered on top. Ladle over hot couscous.

Cloudy Bay Lagoon

Southern calamari

SQUID

Dart Squid *(Nototodarus gouldi)* and **Southern Calamari** *(Sepioteuthis australis)*

If you are fortunate enough to live or overnight on Bruny Island I would suggest that late one evening you dress warmly, turn off all the house lights and take a glass of wine out into the open and look at the sky. Friends who stay with me at Tinderbox say that they have never seen nights of such velvet blackness, nor are the stars closer or larger than here in the south of Tasmania. This is because there is very little artificial light reflecting in the sky and without that urban glow the night sky becomes alive. The Milky Way, the Southern Cross and Venus will help you to find your way around the heavens and, more often than not, you will see a shooting star. If you are very lucky you may see the southern lights, Aurora Australis. Sitting on my verandah, facing due south, I have seen the most amazing displays from the Antarctic horizon, with sheets of red, green and white light pulsating across the sky.

You may ask what this has to do with food; well, there is often another bright light in the sky, so bright that it lights my bedroom at midnight, as if it were day. This light is created by the commercial squid boats that fish Storm Bay and Adventure Bay from Christmas until March. Their bright lights are used to attract the squid to the jigs that catch them.

There are two species of squid caught in Tasmania – the dart squid or Gould's squid, which is a schooling squid; and the southern calamari. The dart squid, although edible, is usually commercially caught and sold as bait fish. It is easily recognised as it has two short fins either side of its body which gives it its characteristic dart shape. The southern calamari has fins that extend down the length of the body and is the fish that recreational fishers are most likely to catch. It is more tender and has more taste. Both species live for only 12 months but are very fast growing and can grow up to two kilograms.

Recreational fishers catch squid in nets, on lines, or they are speared. They are more likely to be caught in shallow bays, inlets and around brightly lit jetties.

Because the squid live for such a short time there is no minimum size but possession is limited to 15 of each variety. They can be taken from all waters around Bruny Island.

The secret for cooking squid is to cook them for a very little time. Pull the legs and head from the body and make sure the transparent plastic-looking quill is discarded. Remove as much of the dark skin and thin membrane as you can. This will make the squid very tender and is worth the effort. The outside flesh can be scored or the tube cut into rings.

SALT AND SZECHUAN PEPPER CALAMARI

Jill's recipe – this is one of the most popular squid recipes and is just delish eaten as nibbles when the hungry hunters return from their fishing trip.

1 calamari

1 tablespoon Szechuan peppercorns

1 tablespoon sea salt

1 teaspoon Chinese five spice

1/3 cup plain flour

1/3 cup corn flour

100 ml iced soda water

Peanut oil for deep frying

Prepare the calamari, score and cut across into two centimetre wide strips – drain on paper towelling.

Heat a small frying pan over high heat with no oil. Roast the peppercorns for a few minutes until they start to pop then remove from the pan. Add the sea salt to the pan and cook over high heat until the salt has turned a grey colour. Grind the salt and pepper mixture with a mortar and pestle until it resembles a fine powder.

Heat a wok with peanut oil over high heat.

Place the cornflour, flour, five spice and the salt and pepper mix into a bowl and add the soda water. Stir until a batter is formed. In small amounts, place the calamari into the batter and pull out over the edge of the bowl leaving just a thin coating of batter. Fry the calamari in small batches until just cooked – approximately 30 seconds. Drain on kitchen paper; serve with lime wedges and your favourite dipping sauce. Eat immediately. Serves four.

CALAMARI WITH A COCONUT CURRY SAUCE

300 ml coconut cream

Zest of one lemon

1 teaspoon grated ginger

2 cloves garlic, crushed

¼ teaspoon powdered saffron

½ teaspoon ground cardamom

1 teaspoon chilli powder

1 teaspoon ground coriander

1 teaspoon ground cumin

1 tablespoon sugar

1 teaspoon salt

1 tablespoon peanut oil

800g calamari

Place all the ingredients in a saucepan except for the calamari. Bring to the boil stirring continuously. Simmer for 15 minutes. Prepare the calamari. Heat the oil in a fry pan until smoking. Add the calamari and stir fry for a minute until curly. Drain on kitchen paper. Add to the sauce and serve immediately on rice with papadams and chutney. Serves four.

Rock formation at Nebraska Beach

HONEY

"I eat my peas with honey,
I've done it all my life,
It makes the peas taste funny,
But it keeps them on the knife". *Anon*

"You never can tell with bees". *A.A. Milne*

"That buzzing noise means something. Now, the only reason for making a buzzing noise that I know of is because you are... a bee! And the only reason for being a bee is to make honey. And the only reason for making honey is so I can eat it". *A.A. Milne*

In the American Museum of Natural History, New York, there is a bee that has been preserved in amber. It is aged at around 100 million years and as such is older than Australia. It is thought that the first bees were solitary and didn't become social creatures until between 10 and 20 million years ago. Then they started congregating and nesting in caves, trees and holes in the ground. There is a cave painting of a hive of bees found in Valencia, Spain, which takes us back in time to 10,000 years ago.

Egyptian hieroglyphics give us plenty of evidence of the domestic use of hives and honey. Barges would take the hives down the Nile and find plants and flowers for the bees to feed on.

The Greeks and Romans were, of course, immensely thorough in their examination of bee behaviour. They used this highly valued product not only as a food source but in many, many other ways. It was used as a 'carb' boost for their Olympic athletes – and still is. Honey was used medicinally, to aid fermentation in making alcohol, as a food preserver and amongst other things, in embalming bodies. When Alexander the Great died thousands of miles from home, his men carried his preserved body back to Macedonia for burial, in a golden coffin filled with honey; an inglorious but sweet homecoming.

Bees were first introduced to Tasmania from Europe in 1831 and since then Tasmanians have developed a thriving and distinctive industry. There are many flavours of Tasmanian bush honey on the market, but Leatherwood honey is outstanding. The bees feed on the leatherwood tree *Eucryphia lucida* which is endemic to Tasmania. This tree grows in great stands, hidden deep in very hard to access areas of our native forests. It is a tree with a simple open white flower that has a very characteristic smell and taste; it is this that makes it so very special. The bees turn the pollen from the leatherwood flower into one of the exceptional natural foods of the world. It has an international reputation as a honey of distinction.

The Wright family from Cradoc are producers of Tasiliquid Gold honey and use Bruny Island as a feeding ground for 60 or more of their 600 hives. The hives are left in four different areas so that the honey from each locality will have a very different flavour. There are leatherwood trees on Mt. Mangana which produce honey with a real taste of Tasmania. I use it a lot in cooking as it imparts its delicious flavour to the food, quite subtly and without too much sweetness.

The prickly box *Bursaria spinosa* growing on the beautiful old property 'Woodlands' at Dennes Point, produces a honey with quite a different taste. Marlene Schmidt who lives on this property keeps half of the honey produced. She sells her award winning Sweet Bursaria honey under the Woodlands label. Her recipe for French walnut and honey tart is just gorgeous.

Manuka honey comes from the tea tree *Leptospermum scoparium* and is widely known for its antibacterial and antifungal properties. It is said that it was named tea tree because Captain Cook used the leaves for his afternoon cuppa!

The fourth of the Wright's Bruny Island production is gathered from an area of land with a miscellany of flowering native bushes, it is loosely termed 'Bush Honey'. Richard and I visited Grahame and his daughter Natalie in a clearing in this bush. These two apiarists have a wonderful rapport with their bees and speak quietly and fondly with them. Grahame was in raptures about the glorious golden colour of the workers as they smothered the frames he was lifting. When he spied the long body of the queen bee, he let out an ecstatic, "God what a beautiful body she has".

I have a new and very healthy respect for bees and their keepers after spending time with these two; the term "as busy as bees" was never more fitting.

There are a few facts that staggered me: the queen bee lays 2000 eggs a day; there are between 25,000 and 30,000 bees in a hive; the drones, whose only job is to mate with the Queen Bee will die after they have done their best; bees fly about 70,000 kilometres to make a pound of honey, that's equivalent to one and a half times around the world. The economic value that bees provide to industry in the form of pollinating fruit trees, vegetables, berry fruits and flowers is valued at AU$188 million in Tasmania. Grahame rather sadly remarked, "No-one seems to acknowledge the good that they do".

However there is a very black cloud on the horizon as Australia is the only honey producing country in the world that is free from that terribly destructive parasitic mite *Varroa destructor*. It is an evil name, for an equally evil creature. It can be totally responsible for the collapse and death of a honey bee colony. At the moment it is hovering around the borders of Australia, as it has already devastated hives in Papua New Guinea, New Zealand, Hawaii and Japan.

The Wright family produces 20 tons of honey in a good year, but say that they could sell 35 tons. We can only hope that this target will be met and that a preventative measure or control will be found before *Varroa destructor* reaches Tasmania, so that we are still able to quote Rupert Brooke – "Stands the church clock at ten to three? And is there honey still for tea?".

FRENCH WALNUT AND HONEY TART

Marlene's recipe – this is a classic French recipe but becomes very Tasmanian by using walnuts that are grown commercially in Tasmania and the local honey.

Sweet shortcrust pastry for tart

175g plain flour

40g castor sugar

125g cold butter, diced

1 egg

1 teaspoon cold water

Filling

100g soft, unsalted butter

100g soft brown sugar

100g Sweet Bursaria honey (other runny honey can be substituted)

100 ml double pouring cream

250g walnuts

4 egg yolks

Put flour, sugar and butter into food processor and whizz until it resembles bread crumbs. Add mixed egg and water to processor whilst still running. Stop as soon as the mixture forms a ball. Roll out the pastry and line a 25 centimetre loose bottomed flan tin and chill for 30 minutes. Heat oven to 180°C. and bake blind for 20 minutes. Remove from the oven.

Melt the butter, sugar and honey together over a low heat, mix gently. Cool slightly until just warm and pour in the cream. Add the walnuts and mix well. Lightly whisk egg yolks and add to the mixture. Pour into the tart base and bake at 180°C. for 30 to 40 minutes or until a glorious shiny dark brown colour. Eat with a slug of crème fraîche or a half and half mixture of thick cream and yoghurt.

GRANOLA

This is a mixed grain and nut cereal that is toasted to a delicious sunny golden brown. I love it sprinkled on top of fresh fruit and plain Greek yoghurt, with a gentle drizzle of honey over the top. It is a great start to the day.

4 cups whole oats

2 cups shredded coconut

½ cup almond flakes

½ cup sunflower kernels

½ cup pepitas

½ cup crushed hazelnuts

¼ cup honey

¼ cup flaxseed oil

Heat oven to 160°C. Combine all the ingredients and spread on a flat baking sheet lined with silicon paper. Bake for 15 minutes or until the mixture is toasted to a golden brown. Cool well before packing into an airtight jar. This mixture will keep for weeks.

HONEY SMOOTHIE

Natalie's recipe – I have used pears, strawberries and leatherwood honey in this recipe, but really any soft fruit or type of honey will make a wonderfully healthy and satisfying drink.

1 cup cold milk

1 cup ripe pear, peeled and de-pipped

6 hulled strawberries

½ cup natural yoghurt

1 tablespoon honey

1 teaspoon ground cinnamon

1 teaspoon ground ginger

6 ice cubes

Blend all ingredients until smooth. Pour into a long glass and drizzle with a little extra honey.

The Neck from North Bruny

MUSSELS

The blue shell mussel *Mytilus edulis*, or common, or black mussel, is one of the oldest species found on earth today and dates back to the beginning of time. This bivalve mollusc is found in inter-tidal waters to depths of 20 metres where they are attached to reefs, rocks, wooden jetty piles and old wharves by their strong, string-like beards. They are distributed throughout the cooler waters of the world and collected and eaten world-wide.

There is an legend that tells of the first cultivation of mussels in the 12th century. A starving, shipwrecked Spanish sailor set up a fishing net on the beach, stretched between two wooden poles. He caught plenty of fish as the tides waxed and waned. After a while he found that mussels were growing on his wooden poles. It was a small and serendipitous beginning to a global industry which now produces more than two million tons of mussels a year and employs 1.5 million people.

These beautiful, elongated, dark blue shellfish were once cultivated on long lines on Bruny Island. They are no longer fished commercially there, but their progeny are just waiting to be collected around most of the jetties and rocks in the bays. Such easy fishing!

When mussels have been collected they should be kept alive, but in a state of hibernation, in the warmest part of your fridge. The vegetable drawer at the bottom covered with a damp towel is ideal.

There is a general misconception that any open mussels should be discarded. This is not so. After you have taken the mussels from your fridge, give them a chance to warm up in the air a bit – say 15 minutes. Then sort through them. Give a tap or squeeze to any that are open – if they don't close, then toss them out. Scrub the shells lightly with a plastic scourer to remove barnacles and crustaceans. This fabulous seafood is now ready to cook.

Place two litres of water with two tablespoons of salt in a large pot and bring to the boil. Cook about a dozen or so mussels at any one time. Cook for exactly one minute. Remove from the water, drain and cool. Some mussels will be open and others may need to be helped. Remove the beard (the hairy bit that anchors the mussel to the rocks). Finally, take a small paring knife, insert the blade in the straight edge of the mussel (where the beard was), and cut the abductor muscle which holds the two shells together. Your mussels are now ready to incorporate into your favourite dish.

If you want half shell mussels, as in the 'whisky butter' recipe, break off the empty shell and toss it out. Leave the mussels whole for the 'creamy mussels in a pot' recipe. After the mussels have been opened they need very little cooking. Over cooked mussels shrink, toughen and become very chewy.

Mussels look very beautiful, have a fabulous flavour and are great value for money, if you have to buy them. They are also known as 'power food' as they are high in protein, vitamin C, zinc, omega 3 and have more iron and vitamin B than beef.

The middens around Bruny Island are evidence of the great number of mussels eaten by the Nuenonne people many thousands of years ago. Bruny D'Entrecasteaux attributed the health and well being of these indigenous islanders to their shell fish diet. He was probably quite right.

CREAMY MUSSELS IN A POT WITH BABY GNOCCHI

Richard told me about the best mussels he had ever eaten when he was visiting Brittany in northern France last year, "they were creamy and had Roquefort cheese in the juice". We practised and came up with this recipe. Richard says it's nearly as good!

4 dozen cooked whole shell mussels

250g cooked baby gnocchi (this can be purchased from most good food shops)

40g butter

1 onion, finely chopped

2 bay leaves

Sprig thyme

500 ml white wine

500 ml fish stock

70g gorgonzola cheese

Salt and pepper

Melt the butter in a large pot over a moderate heat and cook the onion without colouring for about one minute. Add the bay leaf, thyme, wine and fish stock. Bring to the boil and whisk in the crumbled gorgonzola cheese. Add the cooked gnocchi and mussels. Bring to the boil again. Check seasoning and serve immediately into hot bowls and serve with hot, crusty bread.

OYSTERS

Mud Oysters *(Ostrea angasi)* and Pacific Oysters *(Crassostrea gigas)*

There is an ancient fossil-clad rock-shelf on Satellite Island in the D'Entrecasteaux Channel, showing oysters which pre-date human history. The Nuenonne people of Bruny Island had been eating oysters as part of their diet for thousands of years. Huge middens of shells found around the coast of Tasmania, up to three or four metres deep, indicate just how important this food was to them. These native or mud oysters must have been manna from heaven for the early explorers. As Cook wrote in his diary on August 23, 1770, "...mud oysters, these last are the largest and best I ever saw".

These mud oysters were Tasmania's first shellfish export. By the mid 1800's they were shipped to the other Australian colonies and exported, pickled, to New Zealand and Britain, with an annual value of AU$11 million in today's money. Within 60 years, a once healthy industry was completely destroyed by over-fishing, the use of dredges and soil erosion (sediment from the heavy logging on Tasmania's coastline). There is ongoing research into the production of Angasi oysters. There are two commercial licences in Tasmania and the work is still at the experimental stage.

After the Second World War, Pacific oysters were imported from Japan, where there was a flourishing industry. They are now commercially grown all around Tasmania. A new industry was born. The 2012 industry figures show that 3.6 million dozen oysters are consumed each year, Australia wide, with a farm gate value of AU$20 million.

Pacific oysters have a distinctive colour and full bodied flavour, tasting deeply of the sea. Joe and Nicole Bennett have been promoting the nutritional and health benefits of Pacific oysters since 2004. They own one of Tasmania's 70 leases. It is situated in the most stunning position at Great Bay, Bruny Island.

We visited the lease very early one morning in late spring. Joe took us out to the oysters in his super-fast, strong work boat. The morning was perfect. A cloudless, azure sky mirrored in the flat calm waters of the bay, edged by snow capped mountains. It was good to be alive! It was even better when Joe winched the first tray of oysters onto the work boat and started splitting them for us to photograph and taste. There is a succulent crispness in the texture of a just shucked oyster. It lasts for a very short time and then the flesh becomes flaccid and meaningless. The oysters from Great Bay are bathed and fed by the pristine waters of the Southern Ocean in one of the cleanest environments on earth. Joe tells me that an oyster will filter up to 30 litres of water an hour, so their surroundings need to be clean and yet full of nutrients. The government runs a quality shellfish programme and the water is monitored, around the leases, every two weeks, the water in Great Bay is always healthy. The oysters can take from between twelve months to two years to mature, depending on what size is required. This is why the bigger ones are more expensive than the small ones.

Joe's day is long and physical. The up-side of this is that he only has to travel two minutes to get to work and it's a very healthy occupation. It would be hard to imagine a fresher-faced young man, glowing with such good health and intention as Joe. He sells 120,000 dozen oysters a year most of which go to the mainland (Australia). The very freshest are sold at the roadside outlet on North Bruny. You can pull over and eat a dozen there or take some home with you.

It was Joe's choice to stay on Bruny Island and develop a business with his partner Nicole so that they could live in this fabulous environment. One of Joe's catchy sayings is "Oyster Farmer – no drama" and their mission statement is to double the Australian yearly consumption of oysters from six oysters per person each year to twelve. How hard is that?

Adventure Bay Beach

BLOODY MARY SHOOTER

Joe and I agree that the best way to eat an oyster is just out of the water at Great Bay, with a squirt of lemon juice. However, we do need recipes for a cook book. Here is one for Joe:

250 ml tomato juice

80 ml vodka

1 tablespoon Worcestershire sauce

5 drops tabasco sauce

Juice of ½ lemon

Salt and pepper to taste

6 shucked oysters

6 small sticks of celery for stirring and decoration

Put all the Bloody Mary ingredients together in a jug and stir. Keep the cocktail and six shot glasses cold in the refrigerator until you are ready to serve. Pour the cocktail and slip one shucked oyster into each glass. Add a celery stick and serve immediately. Makes six.

VIETNAMESE INSPIRED OYSTERS

Jill's recipe

1 red chilli, thinly sliced

2 tablespoons lime juice

1 clove garlic, crushed

1 tablespoon fish sauce

1 tablespoon rice wine vinegar

2 tablespoons palm sugar

1 tablespoons vegetable oil

2 kaffir lime leaves, finely shredded

100g vermicelli rice noodles

Lebanese cucumber, peeled and cut into thin half slices

Fresh mint leaves

Lettuce leaves to serve

Put the first eight ingredients into a screw top jar and shake well. Let the dressing stand. Break the noodles roughly into four centimetre lengths, put into a bowl, cover with boiling water and allow to stand until soft. Drain and dry on towelling. Take the oysters from their shells and place a small lettuce leaf in the bottom of each empty shell. Put a teaspoonful of noodles onto the leaf and place a whole oyster on top. Add the cucumber and mint leaves and pour over a dessertspoonful of the dressing. Serves four.

WALLABY

Bennett's Wallaby *(Macropus rufogriseus)*
and **Pademelon** or **Rufus Wallaby** *(Thylogale billardieri)*

There are a staggering ten million wallabies in Tasmania – yes, ten million! It's not known how many of them live on Bruny Island but the locals say that it has its fair share. Two species live on Bruny – the more abundant being Bennett's or the Red Nosed Wallaby and, in slightly lesser numbers, the Tasmanian Pademelon or Rufus Wallaby. They both became protected in 1970 when their numbers were depleted due to unregulated hunting. Since then the numbers have tripled, creating conflict with landowners whose crops, pasture and fences they damage. This has now led to sustainable harvesting (hunting) encouraged by the Department of Primary Industries Parks Water and the Environment (hereafter known as DPIPWE).

Richard Clarke has been culling wallaby on Bruny Island for seven or more years. Initially the carcasses were used as pet food, but then Richard learned more about the flesh of this pasture-loving animal. He realised that there was a developing market for a fat free, high protein, low cholesterol, fine quality meat. They graze all day on good pasture and so the flesh is sweet. They are on his door step, so are low in food miles. They do not emit methane gas like sheep, pigs and cattle. In fact, Richard reckons that he is on to a good thing.

As a hunter he must hold a Commercial Wallaby Hunter's Licence which will enable him to shoot wallaby, but he must also work in conjunction with a landholder who has obtained a Crop Protection Permit, also issued by DPIPWE. The cull of wallaby is based on annual spotlight surveys made by the Department. In this way a close watch is kept on their numbers. He has good support from the landowners as he rids them of their problem, but the wallabies are still 'partly protected'.

Three years ago Richard pooled all his resources and bought a beautiful acreage on Bruny Island, where he has built a 'boutique' abattoir. The small custom-built abattoir is situated in the middle of a vast green paddock with stunning views across the D'Entrecasteaux Channel. It is here that he prepares the wallaby, possum, rabbit and hare carcasses for sale to the public.

He value-adds some of the cuts of meat by making chunky wallaby and possum sausages which he spices with local native pepper berries. There is no waste from this product as the skins are all sold and sent away to be tanned. Richard even plucks the exceptionally soft, underbelly fur of the possum, storing it for a time when some entrepreneur will use it to great advantage and create a wonder fibre. Nothing is wasted.

It is a lonely existence for Richard, who usually works by himself. As he looks out over his beautiful acres he dreams of a future where he hopes to share his property with adventurers from the city. He would like to develop cabins, camping grounds and provide outdoor experiences.

Richard's game products can be sourced at the Farm Gate Market, Hill Street Grocer (Augusta Road), Gourmet Butchers and Kingston Town Meats.

GAME SAUSAGES WITH GARLIC MASH AND ONION MARMALADE

Richard Clarke's favourite.

Onion marmalade

1.5 kg onion very thinly sliced

100 ml olive oil

250g brown sugar

50 ml cider vinegar

Stir and toss the onions and oil in a heavy based pan until they are shiny with the oil. Sprinkle brown sugar on top, cover with a lid and stew over a very low heat for two hours. Stir occasionally to prevent sticking. When the bottom layer begins to brown, uncover and stir almost constantly until all the onions have turned a deep golden brown. Pour in the vinegar and turn heat to moderately high. Continue to cook and stir for about 30 minutes, until the onions are a dark and jammy consistency. Pour into warm and sterilized jars and seal. Makes six 250 gram jars.

Garlic mash

4 large Desiree potatoes, peeled and roughly chopped.

3 cloves garlic, peeled

2 ½ cups chicken stock

½ cup cream

100g butter

Salt and pepper, to taste

Boil potatoes, garlic and stock in a pan until tender – about ten minutes. Strain and reserve the broth. Mash the potatoes and garlic adding the butter, cream and stock. If it is necessary, warm again on the stove. The mash will serve four.

WALLABY SHANKS WITH GREMOLATA

Jill's recipe – Bruny Island wallaby shanks tend to be small and tender so you might need two per person.

4 wallaby shanks or 8 if small

½ cup plain flour, seasoned with salt and pepper

2 tablespoons olive oil

6 cloves garlic, peeled

2 leeks cut into 6 cm lengths

1 small head fennel, sliced

6 young carrots, peeled and cut into short lengths

2 parsnips, peeled and cut into short lengths

500 ml red wine

500 ml beef stock

2 tablespoons tomato paste

Dust the shanks in the seasoned flour. Heat the oil in a large heavy based saucepan or metal casserole. Cook the shanks turning them until they are brown all over. Stir in any flour that is remaining. Add the vegetables to the pot and then all the liquid. Stir gently until it boils. Turn the heat down so that the liquid is just simmering. Cook for 90 minutes or until tender. Serve with mashed potato sprinkled with gremolata. Serves four.

Gremolata

This is a classic Italian taste often used as a garnish with veal dishes like Ossobuco. It is usually made with parsley. I sometimes make it with dill to sprinkle on fish dishes, or with rosemary for lamb dishes.

2 cloves of garlic very finely chopped

Grated zest of two lemons

2 tablespoons finely chopped Italian parsley leaves

Combine all ingredients and sprinkle over the wallaby shanks as you serve.

APPLES, PEARS & QUINCES

"With an apple I will astonish Paris". Paul Gauguin

Apples *(Malus domestica)*, Pears *(Pyrus communis)* and Quinces *(Cydonia oblonga)*

As an experiment, William Bligh planted seven apple trees at Adventure Bay in 1788. They were ravaged by fire and only one survived. This experiment was the precursor to one of the most important crops introduced to the island by the early settlers.

Apples were first planted as house orchards (food to be eaten by the family) on Bruny Island, in what could only be called a subsistence economy. From about the mid 1820's onwards there was barely a home without apple, pear and quince trees in the garden, and they did well. The region had plenty of water and was free from disease and pests, so commercial orchards were developed.

Bruny Island became the new place to settle. It was only 11 miles from Hobart and more and more people were buying up land and settling on this idyllic spot.

In 1912 Hobart businessman George Cheverton, was a man who had done well. The colony was flourishing and his bricks were in great demand for the massive amount of building that was happening. He decided to move and run his business from Bruny Island; after all it was only 11 miles from Hobart. I think that in doing this he became one of Hobart's first commuters. He bought Maryville a small house at the southern corner of Great Bay renaming it "Cheverton". He is quoted as having said "What we most want are more settlers of the right sort, who would be good neighbours".

Within a few years George had developed both the land and the house. Revelling in the good soil and growing conditions, he put in 19 acres of fruit trees and grew hay, peas, early potatoes, tomatoes and strawberries. There was no stopping this entrepreneur and as his crops abounded he built his own jetty at the foot of his garden. Packing sheds were developed and steamers would call in to pick up his fruit for Hobart, Sydney and England. Exports peaked in the 1920's and 30's and Tasmania became known, famously, as the "Apple Isle". Hundreds of thousands of tonnes of apples were produced in the channel country. Then the fickle finger of fate beckoned and in 1966 a horrendous hail storm damaged most of the fruit. It could not be sold and most of the crop was destroyed.

This was the beginning of the end for apple growers in what was a typical 'boom-bust' industry. In 1972 England joined the European Common Market and Australia lost most of its apple exports; the Henry Jones IXL Jam Company closed down (they had been using tonnes of fruit in their production) and suddenly the apple industry collapsed. The government assisted growers, who were in financial difficulties by paying them to grub out their trees. This was called "the tree pull scheme", and reduced fruit production by fifty per cent and the numbers of Tasmanian orchardists dropped by 700.

We visited Bev Davis whose family have owned Cheverton since 1943, to pick up some apples, pears and a fabulous basket of quinces to take home. We walked over the property and saw the remains of the once thriving packing shed and the few remaining bleached timbers of the old jetty. Looking across the open paddock, against the sunlight, I could see row upon row of ghostly mounds where once there had been rows of healthy fruit trees. It made me realise how quickly our fortunes can change, often through no fault of our own, and how history is snapping at our heels as we walk through life.

AUTUMNAL DUCK SALAD FOR FOUR

2 large quinces

2 tablespoons honey

1 cinnamon quill

Zest of one lemon

2 duck breasts

2 teaspoons soy sauce

1 tablespoon olive oil

4 cups baby spinach leaves

2 tablespoons olive oil

Salt and freshly ground black pepper

½ cup coarsely chopped, toasted walnuts

4 teaspoons balsamic vinegar

Peel, quarter, and core each quince. Put the quinces, honey, and lemon zest in a heavy based pan. Add enough water to cover the quinces and bring to a boil over medium high heat. Cover the quinces with a piece of grease proof paper and put a firm fitting lid on the saucepan. Reduce the heat to a low simmer and cook until the quinces are dark pink and tender when pierced with a knife, after about 45 minutes. Let them cool in the cooking liquid.

With a very sharp knife score the skin of the duck in a crisscross manner and rub in the soy sauce. Put one tablespoon of olive oil in a heavy based frying pan over a medium heat. Put the duck breasts skin side down in the hot oil and cook for five or six minutes on one side. Then turn them over and cook for four minutes on the other side. Be very careful not to burn them. They should caramelize to a dark brown. Place them on a board to rest before slicing them thinly, at an angle, for the salad.

Toss the spinach and olive oil in a large bowl and season to taste with salt and pepper. Divide the salad evenly among four plates. Slice the quinces and duck breasts and arrange them on each plate. Sprinkle the walnuts on top. Drizzle each salad with one teaspoon of the balsamic vinegar.

Aitkens Point

FISH WITH A CREAM AND APPLE SAUCE (HUON-STYLE)

Jill's recipe – I used Granny Smith apples for this fish dish. They are slightly tart and add acidity to an otherwise rich sauce.

600g of white fish like flathead or winter cod

40g seasoned flour

50g butter

2 apples peeled and sliced

50 ml cider

200 ml cream

1 tablespoon leatherwood honey

Coat the fillets with seasoned flour. Melt the butter in a large heavy based frying pan and pan fry the fish over a moderate heat for two minutes each side until a light golden brown. Keep the fillets warm. Pan fry the apple slices and add cider, cook until apples are tender. Add the honey and cream; season to taste. Cook over a moderate heat until the sauce begins to thicken. Add the fish to the sauce. Serve on rice with a salad. Serves four.

PEAR SORBET WITH SWEET PEAR CRISPS

Pear sorbet

5 ripe sweet pears (William) peeled, cored and sliced

¾ cup Riesling

¾ cup sugar

2 tablespoons lemon juice

Bring all the ingredients to the boil and cook until the pears are soft. Cool and put into a blender and blitz until the mixture is smooth. Put in a shallow dish in the freezer. Every half an hour, for the next couple of hours, take the dish out of the freezer and whisk up the mixture. An easier way is to use an ice cream maker. Make at least two hours before you want to eat this sorbet. Serves six.

Sweet pear crisps

2 pears

2 tablespoons raw sugar

Heat oven to 160°C. Wash two pears and cut into extremely thin slices. I use the thinnest blade of a mandolin and it is just perfect. Put two tablespoons raw sugar onto a plate and coat each side of the pear. Place the pear slices on baking paper on a flat oven tray and cook for 15 minutes each side. Completely cool on a wire rack and store in an airtight jar.

CHEESE

Bruny Island Cheese Co.

Nick Haddow is a relative latecomer to Bruny Island. He first visited as a tourist, whilst making cheese at the Pyengana Cheese Factory, and fell totally in love with the place. He bought a one hundred year old picturesque, but rather sadly dilapidated house, resting in a field full of poppies and daisies. I don't know how many people have driven past that house (me included) and fantasised about a sea change in their lives, imagining creating a thing of beauty out of the pile of old, grey, weather-beaten boards and toppling verandahs. Well, Nick and his family did.

Nick has built the cheese factory next door to his now, newly painted and happy home. The Cheese Co. is where Nick works like a dervish at his craft – or is it a science? He is a true Renaissance man who has spent many years travelling in Europe, studying the ancient history of cheese production with seasoned artisans, but it is here in Tasmania that Nick makes distinctive cheeses with flavours and textures that are characteristic of the area and are not mass produced. He does not cling to the European traditions but is laying the foundations of a new genre of cheese.

For the seven years that the Cheese Co. has been in operation Nick has created a fantastic reputation for himself and his range of nine different cheeses. He tells me that eighty percent of his cheeses are sold either through the farm gate or through his Cheese Club – it is an enviable position to be in as it means that he sells most of his cheeses at their absolute optimum for eating.

I can't say that I have any one particular favourite cheese, but I do absolutely adore several of them; C2 is a hard, cloth-covered cheese made from unpasteurised milk in traditional wooden hoops – the first of its kind made in Australia. Its rind is wiped every week to encourage the surface bacteria to do their work, giving the cheese a clean, sweet, nutty flavour. This is a cheese to be eaten simply, as it is, but it can also be grated and used in many cooked dishes.

The Saint, another favourite of mine, is a soft, creamy, oozy, cheese which develops quite a bite with age. It is delicious eaten with one of the sour dough loaves baked in the Cheese Co.'s wood fired oven.

Perhaps my most favoured is the soft cheese named "1792", reminding us of the year that Bruny D'Entrecasteaux first set foot on this island. These small cheeses mature on Huon Pine boards and are regularly hand washed in brine to enhance the strong flavour and aroma. They are robust, pungent and earthy – what my family call "soxy" cheese.

It seems almost a sin to suggest cooking Nick's cheeses that look and taste stunning as they are, perfectly aged and ready to eat. In consequence, Nick's favourite recipe is so simple that it hardly needs writing down. It is, as he says, for Sunday night – fast and easy when there's probably not much left in the fridge and is always a favourite with the children.

A HAPPY FAMILY MEAL – PASTA WITH CHEESE

Nick's recipe – cook enough pasta for the family. When cooked add salt, pepper and a bright little Tasmanian olive oil. If you have any herbs or interesting leaves in the garden tear them up and put them in at this stage. Serve with mounds of grated C2 cheese.

SICILIAN CHEESE TART

Jill's recipe – this recipe is a little more involved and makes a gorgeous lunch or picnic dish served with a crispy green salad. The lardy pastry is especially good in this recipe.

Marsala pastry

500g plain flour

150g soft lard

1 egg

125 ml Marsala

Salt and pepper

Filling

500g fresh ricotta cheese

200g grated C2 Cheese or strong cheddar

150g double smoked bacon with the rind removed and cut into thin strips

2 eggs

Preheat the oven to 200°C. You will need a greased 23 centimetre loose bottomed flan or cake tin.

In a food processor, mix the lard into the sifted flour. Add the egg and Marsala and blitz until a soft, pliable dough forms – add a little cold water if necessary. Roll out two thirds of the pastry and line the pan so that the pastry comes up the sides and a little over the top.

Beat the two eggs lightly and mix all the filling ingredients together. Add ground black pepper. You will most likely not need salt as the bacon and cheeses are quite salty in themselves. Pour the mixture into the pastry dish then roll out the remaining pastry into a round circle to cover the dish. Seal the edges with your fingers and prick the surface with a fork. Place in a hot oven and bake for 40 minutes or until a delicious golden colour.

Allow to cool completely and set before cutting the pie. Serves four.

OLIVES & PEPPER BERRIES

Mountain Pepper Berry *(Tasmannia lanceolata)* and the **Wild Olive** *(Olea europaea)*

Olive production is new to Bruny Island and relatively new to Australia. There are over 17 million tonnes of olives produced worldwide each year, and Australia doesn't even rate in the twenty top producing countries. Matthew's olive grove is new. He planted nine hundred and sixty young trees just ten years ago, on a well drained, north-facing slope in the hills behind Adventure Bay. It's just a small clearing in a lush Tasmanian bush paradise on the lower slopes of Mount Mangana. The olive trees, mostly the Arecuzzo variety, have settled well into their new environment and this year promises to be abundant. The small, green olives glisten and shine, hanging from the healthy trees "like chains of pearls", Matthew remarks.

As we walked around Matthew's property, admiring one of the biggest chestnut trees I have ever seen, he told us a story about another enormous tree. In 1890, Ted Murray senior and Ted Murray junior were timbermen living here on this property, working and felling the eucalypts on Mount Mangana. John Watt Beattie, a famous Hobart photographer, had made the full day's journey to Adventure Bay for the occasion and had taken their photograph with two other timbermen, felling a forest giant. It was an iconic photograph. In 1930, Treasury was asked to produce a new twenty pound note to celebrate the timber industry. They chose the photograph of the tree-felling at Adventure Bay to go on the reverse side of the new note. It was a case of fame but no fortune.

As we walked we heard a shrill screaming bird that we couldn't identify. The laugh was on us – it was a bird scarer. The machine, working off a solar panel, is used to keep the Tasmanian Black Currawongs at bay. These yellow eyed, raven-black birds are lured by the fragrant scent of the Mountain Pepper Berry bushes that are planted around the farmhouse. They would have a picnic with their huge black beaks if it weren't for the mechanical, piercing screech that keeps them away.

The Mountain Pepper has its origins in Gondwanaland. It has very distinctive shiny, green, aromatic leaves and red stems. The small cream flowers develop into dark brown berries, which will dry out to look just like the black pepper we are used to, except that the native berry is hotter and with more fragrance.

It has been used as both food and medicine by the indigenous people, who always seemed to recognise a good thing, as the berries are full of antioxidants.

The dried berries can be put in a pepper grinder to add a little extra zing to the usual grind. They can also be used to infuse soups, stews, sauces, vinegar and drinks. Matthew tells me he puts them into his home brew – it makes the beer pink with vitality.

We drove on to Lueena, another olive grove a few kilometres back along the road towards the ferry.

Owen and his wife Dianne called the olive grove Lueena, it is the indigenous name for the Superb fairy wren *(Malurus cyaneus)*. This relatively tame, dainty little bird is found in the bush around the olive grove. It can be spotted by the sudden flashes of brilliant, cyan-blue wings of the male bird. In family groups they flit into the grove and remove unwanted bugs and insects from around the trees.

What a lovely name to give your property.

Owen bought the land in 2002 and immediately planted 140 olive trees. He insists that Dianne is the gardener, and he is her lackey, but they both seem to be in this business together. Owen, who has been involved with the development of the farmed salmon industry, brings a scientific background to their project. This can be seen by the meticulous order and discipline evident in the grove. It is a delight, with healthy fruit laden trees, on a slight incline, bathed in sunlight.

They have put a system in place that waters and fertilizes the trees at set times. This fertigation system has probes set around each trees roots to assess when nourishment and water is needed. This saves the tree from being over watered and over fed. They have been bearing fruit for some years now, but won't reach real commercial production for at least another three years.

Several varieties of olive tree have been planted, mostly Manzanilla (little apple), a Spanish variety which is widely grown for its high yield of oil. There are small Ligurean olives to be used as table fruit and a very special variety of olive, with a scent and taste of roses – or perhaps it's Turkish delight. I really can't wait to taste that one. Olives are remarkably versatile and further varieties are being planted to ascertain which ones best suit this part of the world.

Owen and Dianne have a brilliant operation, but as one can imagine, the financial drain has been massive. They are indeed pioneers, and as my old father in law Hargrave-Wilson used to say, "Pioneering don't pay – but may just pave the way for future generations". Their produce is available at The Cheese Co.

BUSH PEPPER INFUSED VINEGAR

4 tablespoons pepper berries

1 litre white vinegar

Bring the vinegar to the boil and pour it over the berries. Stand for three or four weeks. Strain through a coffee filter into bottles. Use in dressings and marinades it is a fabulous colour.

OLIVE, ONION AND ANCHOVY BREAD

This popular bread recipe is also known by many other names – the Italian pizza, Sicilian sfincione (focaccia), French pissaladière and Niçoise tart. It is just wonderful under any name and makes a great addition to a barbecue or as a lunchtime dish with salad.

Bread recipe

500g pizza flour

1 tablespoon salt

1 tablespoon dried yeast

400 ml warm water

1 tablespoon olive oil

Topping for bread

2 red onions, sliced

2 tablespoons olive oil

20 pitted olives

20 anchovy fillets, drained on paper towelling

200g rough grated cheese

Fresh rosemary leaves

You will need a rectangular baking tray approximately 35 x 22 centimetres. Oven at 220°C.

Place flour, salt and yeast in a large bowl and mix in water and oil. Knead for ten minutes. It may be easier for you to do this on a well-floured table. When the dough is soft and elastic and no longer sticky, place it back into a well-floured bowl and cover with cling film. Put in a warm place to rise for about one hour. Turn the risen dough on to a floured work surface and flatten with the heel of your hand. Knead for a few minutes. Roll out and fit into a well-oiled baking tray.

While the bread dough is proving, cook the onions gently in the oil without browning them. Cool and spread over the dough. Press the olives into the bread and place the anchovies between the olives. Sprinkle over the rosemary leaves and cover with grated cheese. Bake for half an hour.

Owen and Dianne's shack on their property Lueena

CHOCOLATE

"Paradise without people is not worth setting foot in". *An old Arabic saying*

An unlikely couple, a dentist and a chocolatier, have created their own paradise on Bruny Island. Twenty five acres of rolling green parkland lead down to the edge of Adventure Bay. Here one can gaze out to the very spot where the good ship Adventure, a Whitby collier of 335 tons, first dropped anchor in 1773. It was captained by Tobias Furneaux whose purpose was to accompany James Cook on his second Voyage of Discovery. He named Adventure Bay after his ship. Penguin Island at the north-east corner of the bay was named after the rare yellow-crested penguins that inhabited those rocks and Quiet Corner because of "the sheltering effect of the high stone cliff" at Fluted Cape.

Looking down from the cliff-top across the tessellated pavements into the clear, crystalline waters of Storm Bay, one views a primitive sea and landscape image that hasn't changed since 1773 – a Furneaux snapshot.

The dentist and the chocolatier built Hiba, which is an Arabic word meaning "a gift from God". This captivating, finial-topped building became both their home and chocolate factory.

Fifteen years of incredibly hard work, love and enormous fun has developed the Hiba Estate into a thrilling, eventful and unique lifestyle for Bob and Michael. The lake, follies, rose gardens, rhododendron walks and kitchen garden are in an annual metamorphosis – blooms and blossoms ever changing.

Chocolate making is the heartbeat of Hiba in the huge and magnificent purpose-built kitchen. Ten varieties of chocolate fudge, chocolate sauces and truffles are prodigiously manufactured in this, the hub of the house.

It all started when Michael was working as a pâtissière at the Hyde Park Hotel in London. Fudge making was part of his daily routine, but it was divinely creamy fudge that he made, not at all like the usual vigorously beaten, crunchy fudge. His chef, Englishman John Insley, allowed him to bring the fudge recipe back to Australia – the only changes made were to incorporate local ingredients, making the fudge a genuinely Australian product. These addictive and gorgeous chocolate goodies are sold in the Bruny Island Providore, nationally and in most specialist food outlets in Tasmania.

Michael and Bob open the Hiba garden to the public at appointed times during the year. If you are lucky, your visit to Bruny Island might just coincide with an open garden day.

HIBA MESS

Michael's recipe – this is Hiba's variation of Eton Mess, a traditional dessert eaten at the annual Eton versus Winchester cricket match in England. The recipe has one of Michael's fudge bars melted through it, giving it a rich and luxurious twist.

1 bag of Tasmanian Company Baby Meringues or use home-made meringues broken into small pieces

2 punnets strawberries, hulled and cut in half

2 cups of cream

95g bar chocolate fudge (I like the hazelnut flavoured one in this dish)

Melt the Tasmanian Fudge Company's fudge bar in half a cup cream over a gentle heat. Cool – this should become a thick glossy chocolate sauce. Whip the rest of the cream to form thick peaks. Place the meringues in a large bowl and gently fold in half of the cream, then the chocolate sauce. Add the strawberries and lightly fold in the rest of the whipped cream. Place this 'mess' on a serving dish or in individual bowls and spoon over the rest of the chocolate sauce. Serves six.

CHOCOLATE FRIANDS

Jill's recipe – friands are a very rich and splendid sort of cup cake and they are just delicious with coffee. The name 'friand' comes from the French word 'friandises' which means a little sweet delicacy to be eaten with the fingers. I use the orange flavoured fudge bar for this recipe.

6 egg whites

80g plain flour

250g icing sugar

120g ground almond meal

175g melted butter

95g bar Tasmanian Fudge, grated or finely chopped

Preheat oven to 190°C. Oil a 12 portion friand tin. Whisk egg whites lightly until just frothy. Sift flour and icing sugar into another bowl and add almond meal. Stir the egg whites and melted butter into the flour mix then fold in the finely grated fudge. Divide mixture between the 12 recesses in the tin and bake for 25 minutes – done when tested with a wooden skewer and it comes out clean. Cool for four minutes before turning out. Dust with castor sugar. Eat warm. Heavenly!

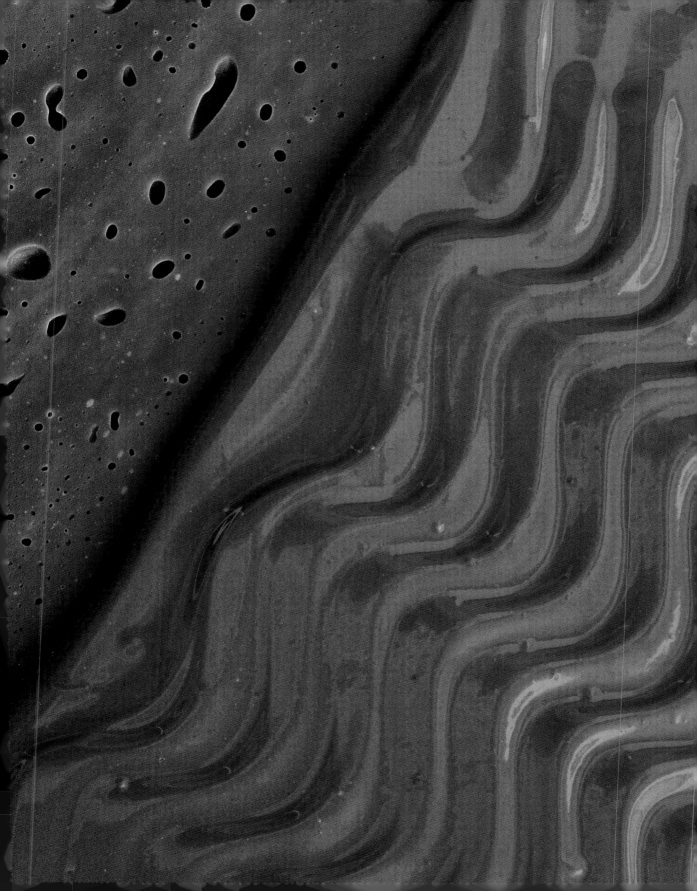

BERRY FRUITS

Bruny Island Berry Farm

Adventure Bay from the earliest of times was known for its clean, fresh, drinking water. The early explorers queued up to refill their water barrels and stock up for their long voyages out into the Pacific. Captain Tobias Furneaux in 1773, Captain James Cook in 1777 and ten years later Captain William Bligh, all noted taking water from the "Watering Place". It was later renamed Resolution Creek by Bligh, after Cook's vessel Resolution, which was used in his second and third voyages of discovery.

Rain continues to fill Resolution Creek and in doing so provides nutrient-rich, flood plains for Kathryn and Graham O'Keefe's berry farm. The original farm, Highwood, has belonged to Kathryn's family since settlement in the 1880s. Her ancestor, Lars Hansson, came out from Sweden in 1885. He and his wife Augusta had only fourteen children, but Lars himself came from a family of twenty children. His mother was honoured by the King of Sweden, who upon learning of this wonderful woman's success in helping populate the little country town, gathered all the children together at his palace, for a royal photograph. It still hangs in the National Museum in Sweden.

The Hansson family continued to thrive and populate Tasmania. They became well known and well respected families in the south.

Kathryn received a gift of 30 acres of Highwood from her father. After a great deal of thought they decided to plant nine different varieties of berries. She and Graham call the property Woodleigh and encourage visitors to picnic or just commune with nature and the waterbirds on the dam. Not only can you pick your own fruit but the kitchen produces a gorgeous berry cake, as well as stunning pancakes filled with strawberries and raspberries, cream and ice cream. A local favourite are the little jewel-like berries in sparkling, champagne jelly which is an absolute delight. The locals have been known to buy half a dozen or more at a time of these delicious desserts, as a take away for a special dinner party. Kathryn has generously given me the recipe to print in this book. I made one for my family's Christmas dinner in a huge glass bowl. By golly it was good!

The farm shop is packed with 'berry' goodies. There are jams, vinegars, honey, sauces, toys, cards, clothing and anything that has a picture of a berry on it! Sitting soaking up the ambience and warmth of the land, you may just find that you are sitting next to Kathryn's father – and he has plenty of stories to tell.

BERRIES IN CHAMPAGNE JELLY

Kathryn's recipe

1 bottle of Champagne

2 cups sugar

2 tablespoons or 6 leaves of gelatin

6 cups fruit (blueberries, raspberries, sliced strawberries)

200 ml runny cream for the top

Place the Champagne and sugar into a saucepan and bring to the boil stirring occasionally.

Remove from heat and allow to cool until just warm. Mix gelatin with half a cup of boiling water and stir until dissolved. Add gelatin to Champagne syrup then add fruit.

Ladle into glasses. Fill approximately eighty per cent allowing for cream on top. Refrigerate to set. Serves six .

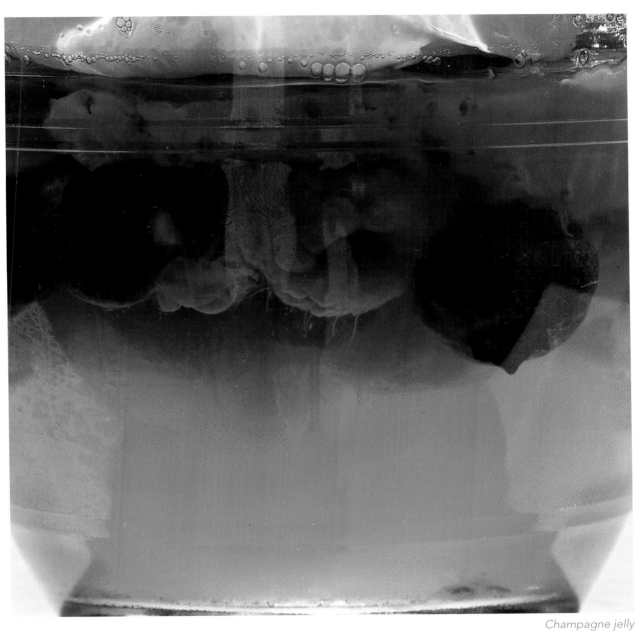

Champagne jelly

MOIST TASSIE BERRY CAKE

Jill's recipe – you can use frozen berries, but this is really a recipe for summer when the fruit is fresh and ripe. The yoghurt in the recipe ensures a good moist cake.

2 cups mixed berries, any mixture of raspberries, strawberries, blue berries, blackberries

3 cups self raising flour

100g soft butter

2 cups castor sugar

3 eggs

1 cup yoghurt

Grated zest from 1 orange

You will need a greased 23 centimetre spring form pan and your oven at 180°C. Combine berries and coat gently with the flour. Cream soft butter and sugar adding the eggs one at a time. Fold the yoghurt and orange zest into this mixture (at this stage it looks a bit like scrambled eggs but don't worry it will come good). Fold in the flour and fruit until thoroughly mixed. Bake for one hour and test with a skewer for doneness. Dust with icing sugar and eat warm with a dollop of cream or yoghurt.

Replica Bark Endeavour approaching Cape Queen Elizabeth in Adventure Bay
Opposite: Copy of Captain Cook's chart published in France

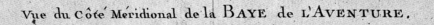

Vue du Côté Méridional de la BAYE de l'Aventure.

I. Penguin

PLAN
DE LA BAYE DE L'AVENTURE
sur la
TERRE VAN-DIEMEN.

Lat. 43.21.20. S. Long. 147.25. E. Décl. 5.15 E. 1777.

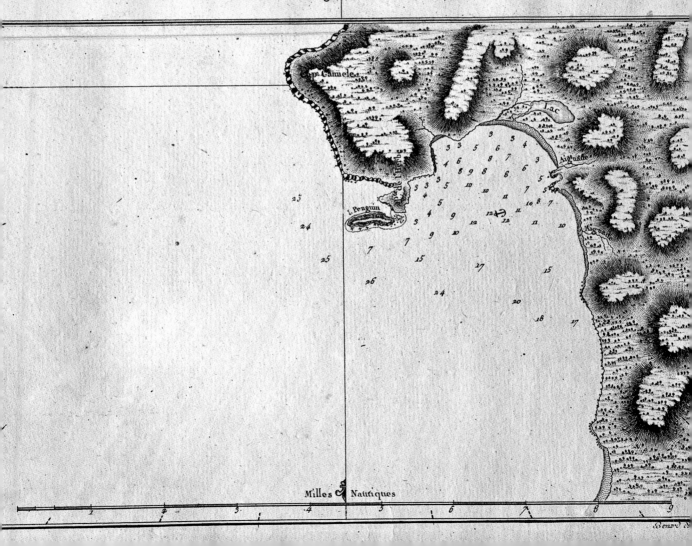

Cap Cannelé

Lac

I. Penguin

Aiguade

Milles Nautiques

Benard d.

ABALONE

Blacklip Abalone (*Haliotis rubra*) and **Greenlip Abalone** (*Haliotis laevigata*)

My two young friends, Mia and Noah, are real water babies and just love snorkeling around the coastal waters of Bruny Island. Like most young, they don't seem to feel the cold and now that wet suits come in all sizes they can spend even longer in the water. One of their greatest joys is searching for abalone – the hunter gatherer instinct seems to be lurking in us from a very young age. Young Noah looked at me incredulously when I told him that I had read about Nuenonne women diving for shellfish and staying down under the water for at least fifteen minutes.

The abalone, sometimes called mutton fish, is found in waters all around the Tasmanian coast. Tasmania's commercial divers produce approximately twenty five per cent of the world's abalone harvest which is boosted by stock from abalone farms in Tasmania.

The D'Entrecasteaux Channel is open only to recreational divers who gather blacklip abalone. A potential diver will first have to buy a licence, learn the size limit and then know how to find the beastie. The recreational season is open all year round with a daily bag limit of ten abalone and a possession limit of twenty. Noah and Mia don't have any trouble finding their quota every time they dive for a meal but they have been working their 'patch' for some years. Fisheries tell us that 12,500 Tasmanians recreationally fish for abalone, so one must be, like these children, sparing with their catch, being considerate to the long term viability of the species.

This marine gastropod has the most beautifully shaped shell. From above it looks like a rock in the water, but the underside of the shell is a perfect ear composed of mother-of-pearl. This iridescent nacre has been collected over many centuries by many cultures and used as a decoration on furniture, musical instruments, jewelry and buttons.

Abalone do not move about much but instead fix themselves more or less to one spot where the algae drift is good. The algae-rich seawater filters through the abalone's gills, where it is taken in, digested, and then escapes through a series of holes around the edge of the shell.

The large foot, which it uses to cling to the rock, provides the meat that we eat. The abalone needs to be prised away from its habitat with a bar or long bladed knife and a certain amount of strength. It is always wise to measure the shell under water before pulling it away from its home. Damaged abalone left in the water can bleed to death (use the DPIPWE "Recreational Sea Fishing Guide" for all information).

Scientists have predicted that wild abalone will become extinct within the next 200 years at the current rate of acidification of our oceans; another wake up call.

Mia and Noah are indeed fortunate to have had Cloudy Bay and the lagoon as their adventure playground since they were born. Fishing and caring for the biodiversity surrounding them, has become second nature. Their eyes gleam as they talk about living close to the water, fishing, swimming and snorkeling. Their parents have been instrumental in teaching them to recognise the fragility of their environment. Many years ago their father, Rob, was a commercial fisherman. As he fished around Bruny Island he realized that the island's true beauty was far more evident from the sea than from the land and that he would like to share this with others.

During 1999, in a very brave move, Rob sold his fishing boat and started Pennicott Wilderness Journeys. It is adventure tourism at its very best. The purpose-built yellow rubber boats take tourists out from Adventure Bay and travel south past the fantastic Fluted Cape. The boat hugs the sea cliffs allowing the passengers to truly appreciate the coastline and natural rock formations of this rugged paradise.

It is a bird watchers heaven. The skies are often full of petrels, gannets, terns, shearwaters and albatross. At the top of my list is the great wandering albatross, the sea eagle and the Dominican gull – I have seen them all. As the yellow boat travels south there is a point at which the skipper of your boat announces that you are now in the Southern Ocean. Looking down towards the southern ice shelf the view is uninterrupted and there is a sudden, mysterious chill in the air.

Friars Rocks are the most southerly point of Bruny island. Here an immense seal haul-out will greet you with the graceful creatures slipping into the sea to roll, dip and dive around the boat. I have also seen immense pods of dolphins out in Storm Bay. Occasionally one will be lucky enough to see a Southern Right whale on its journey around the bottom of Tasmania making its way to warmer seas.

The road has been a long and hard one for Rob and his family but it has been a meteoric ride. It is his undaunted passion to spare and share the environment with others that drives Rob forwards. There are now six boats in the fleet, all manned by enthusiastic, knowledgeable, passionate young seafarers. Rob was named the 2012 Tasmanian, Australian of the Year and his Bruny Island Cruise named the Best Tourist Attraction in Tasmania. I have yet to meet a tourist who hasn't rated this eco-journey one of the best in the world.

PREPARING ABALONE

This can be quite tricky. Cook very briefly. Some recipes will tell you that abalone can be steamed very slowly and cooking times vary from between 20 minutes and six hours. I have tried twice and found the meat always to be bland-tasting and very chewy, even rubbery! I am not prepared to use one of Australia's most highly valued seafoods as an experiment anymore. The following recipe is the only one I will ever use for this delicacy. Young Mia agrees with me here. In fact she likes her abalone raw, thinly sliced and eaten with wasabi and soy sauce.

Remove the meat from the shell with a blunt knife or spatula. Cut away the guts and trim all surfaces free of any dark skin. Scrub well in cold salted water. This process is much better performed in the sea so that all the debris can be eaten by the small fish and there is no wastage. Slice the meat of the abalone horizontally into very thin slices, about two millimetres thick. Pound the slices between sheets of plastic film with a mallet. The fish is now ready for cooking.

SWIFTLY COOKED ABALONE

Heat two tablespoons of butter in a wide flat frying pan. When the butter is bubbling cook abalone for twelve seconds each side. No longer or it will become tough. It is better to cook in several small batches. Serve immediately with squeezed lemon.

Resolution Creek at Adventure Bay

RECREATIONAL FISHING

"The charm of fishing is that it is the pursuit of what is illusive but attainable, a perpetual series of occasions for hope". *John Buchan*

This is a first rate definition of recreational fishing from the famous author of "The Thirty-Nine Steps", John Buchan. It is the pursuit of "what is illusive but attainable", that gives the keen fisher the urge to go back again and again. The pure waters around Bruny Island offer a wonderful opportunity to access a wide range of very popular species. Statistics tell us that more than one in four Tasmanians fish in salt water each year. Fishing is a recreation that is not just for catching fish; it is relaxation; it is time spent with mates or family; it is enjoyment of the whole marine environment; it is the anticipation and preparation of an exceptional day with an unknown ending.

As dawn breaks over the D'Entrecasteaux Channel, the silence is broken by the buzz of tinnies speeding over the wide waterway. The fishers are all on a mission and have the great expectation that today will be 'the day'.

Tasmania is renowned for sudden weather changes blowing in from the west and believe me, it can blow. As Richard says, "it's blowing hard enough to blow dogs off chains". I have known the weather change from flat calm to gale force within minutes. However settled the dawn may seem, it is essential to be prepared before leaving the safety of home. Do please ring MAST (Marine and Safety Tasmania) for a boating weather update. You will always find a sheltered shore or bay on Bruny Island regardless of the weather conditions, but it is frightening and tough to be caught unawares and unprepared, on the water in a storm.

The range of fish species around Bruny Island is wide and varied. There are mussels, oysters, clams and abalone just waiting to be picked out of the water – if you know where to look. The beaches and many wooden jetties are home to wrasse, flathead and leatherjackets. Calamari and Gould's squid appear in abundance in the early summer. The isthmus or Neck Beach is a great area for surf fishing with Australian (black back) salmon, gummy, school shark, sand flathead and rays for the offering. There are bays, where at night, by torchlight, flounder can be speared. Fishers in boats with nets, lines and pots have the opportunity to catch crayfish, barracouta, bream, mullet, pike, Australian salmon, flathead, cod, and sea-run trout.

The deeper waters south of Bruny Island can occasionally produce such marvels as striped trumpeter and yellow fin tuna. It is suggested that the very best fishing spot for striped trumpeter is in the waters around Pedra Branca, which is south of Bruny Island.

Recreational fishers may give away their catch, but they cannot sell or barter their fish. Only commercial fishers with commercial licences are able to sell. It is a good maxim to fish responsibly; take only what you can eat; use good technique; be considerate of the environment and others; treat the fish gently.

The Department of Primary Industries, Parks, Water and Environment fondly known as DPIPWE provide a free pamphlet "Recreational Sea Fishing Guide". This little book is just excellent and is essential for any fisher. It outlines all the marine fishing rules and includes information regarding which licences are needed, area closures and restrictions, size, possession and bag limits. It also provides a little 'insider information' as to where you might catch whichever species of fish you are after. The informative booklet can be picked up from all Service Tasmania outlets and is available on the internet at www.fishing.tas.gov.au/licence.

Marine fishing rules have been set in place to stop our waters from being over fished. I feel that the rules are over generous and the bag limits often too liberal. Instead of thinking in the terms of 'bag limits', perhaps to take only what your family can eat would be more acceptable. Domestic freezers bulging with fish that will never be eaten (except perhaps by the dog) and bragging comments such as, "oh, we caught over a hundred flounder last night" is simply not on. It is up to us to see that our grandchildren have the same opportunity to put the 'Gone Fishin' sign up over their doors.

Smoked couta

D'Entrecasteaux Channel, Mt. La Pérouse and Pindars Peak

FLATHEAD

Two old friends in a red dinghy is the epitome of mateship. It is a time and place for relaxation and camaraderie, where the worries of real life can melt away. Rob and Keith share a shack at Snake Bay. Seen from the outside it's an unpretentious green shed, but like so many sheds on Bruny Island it hides a bijou and well designed interior. There are all the essentials, with electricity, fresh rain water tanks, a fully functional loo, two bedrooms, television, sound system, books galore, a wood fire and an endless supply of beer in the fridge. It is both heaven and haven with all the home comforts.

Rob who lives in Sydney bought the property as an investment for his family. He is unable to be there very much, but his mates Keith and Carolyn are the best caretakers in the world. They can frequently be seen fishing in Snake Bay, shopping at the Bruny Island market or kicking up their heels at the musical evening at Alonnah; one could say that they have embraced the Bruny Island lifestyle with a passion.

Fishing in Snake Bay can be satisfying but not brilliant; nevertheless, it is one of life's simple pleasures. More often than not the catch will be the ubiquitous flathead (*Platycephalus bassensis*) who are so cooperative that they will give themselves up to a bent pin. Did you know that Tasmanians catch over two million flathead each year, but since the catch and release technique has been recommended, forty per cent of these are now returned to the water. Even though some of these returned fish die, it is infinitely preferable to seeing piles of rotting fish left on the beach. This was once quite a common occurrence.

There are several species of flathead caught in these waters, but more often than not, it will be sand flathead that comes up on your line. They are designed for living on the sea floor where they bury themselves into the sandy bottom until just their eyes can be seen. They are carnivorous creatures and will lie in wait for a passing prey to swim past, and then, rising out of the sand, will snap it up. They are armed with ridges of sharp and slightly poisonous spines; although the venom is not fatal it can cause a lot of pain to the unwary fisher. The wound will feel better if washed with vinegar. This is the most populous fish targeted by amateur fishermen and one of the most popular eating fish. I think it is because eating it reminds you of the first time you ever caught a fish (most likely a flathead).

There is a small inexpensive home smoker available on the market that smokes small amounts of fish just perfectly. It is about twice the size of a shoebox and ideal for home, boat, caravan or wherever. I cannot recommend it highly enough but the secret is to use dry, hardwood shavings. Pine will give the fish a very bitter taste. We used it to smoke the flathead fillets for the fish pie and Richard experimented with couta fillets. It added a certain 'je ne sais quoi' to what can be, in my mind a rather ordinary fish. Especially when served with lashings of his homemade hollandaise sauce. Minimum size is 30 centimetres with a possession limit of 30 fish.

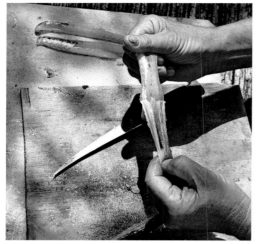

Keith has an unusual filleting method shown in the photographs here.

Hold the fish by the head and with your very sharp filleting knife cut down along the backbone almost to the end of the tail.

Separate the fillet from the skin for almost two thirds of the length of the fish.

Then pull the flesh away from the fish, separating the bones from the fillet.

Turn the fish and proceed in exactly the same way on the other side of the fish.

You will end up with boneless fillets and a fishy, head-on skeleton.

The head and bones will make a great fish stock, but at Snake Bay there are quolls and sea eagles who love Keith's fishy castoffs.

FISH PIE

Flathead are very versatile and can be cooked by all methods. The recipe here is chosen because the flathead fillets smoke so beautifully. We make it often, and it is fondly known as Sheepwash Bay Pie.

1 kg potatoes for mashing

60g butter

100 ml milk

6 hard boiled eggs

500g white skinless and boned fish fillets like flathead

500g hot smoked fish (can be bought from your fishmonger)

1 cup white wine

500 ml milk

80g butter

80g flour

100g grated tasty cheese

Handful parsley finely chopped

50g capers

Salt and pepper

You will need six individual or one large oven proof dish.

Mash one kilogram cooked potatoes with warm milk and butter until soft and creamy, add salt and pepper. Hard boil six eggs and cut each egg into quarters.

Poach the unsmoked fish in a mixture of white wine and milk. Add a little salt and pepper to taste and a bay leaf or two, if you have them. Cook gently by bringing the mixture to the boil and then remove from heat. Take fish out of the liquid and drain. Break all the fish into smallish pieces mixing in the smoked fish.

For the béchamel (white sauce), make a roux with melted butter and plain flour then stir in the liquor from the cooked fish. Bring to the boil adding enough extra milk to make a good thick sauce. Add grated tasty cheese, (reserve a handful for the top of the pie), a handful of chopped parsley, and 80 grams baby capers. Test for salt and pepper. Pour this rich delicious sauce over the smoked and poached fish and eggs in an oven proof dish. Spread the mashed potatoes evenly over the fish – smooth the surface of the potato and make patterns with the tines of a fork. Brush with a little melted butter and sprinkle over the remaining cheese. Bake on a high shelf at 180°C. for 30 to 40 minutes or until thoroughly heated through and browned on top. I have made the pies in little individual pots. It will make six.

Serve with a green leafy salad. It will serve four hungry hunters or six normal folk.

WINTER COD

Winter Cod or **Bearded Rock Cod** (*Pseudophycis barbata*)

Winter Cod or Southern Rock Cod are plentiful in the Bruny Island waters. They are caught on rods, in nets and in traps. They are foolishly dismissed by some as "slippery little buggers" and not worth eating. The flesh is white and soft but cooked with a little 'know how' they are very pleasant.

One of the reasons that some fishers don't like them, is that their bodies are covered with a mucous film when they come out of the water. This slime is a defence mechanism used to prevent other predators from latching on to them. Tasmanians, with a rather over-obvious use of the vernacular refer to them as 'slimies'. One of the advantages of this cod, which is in no way related to the real cod, *(gaddus)*, is that there is no size limit and they can grow up to six kilograms in weight. These large fish can be as old as seven or eight years.

The fish is bicoloured, being reddish-brown on top and a pale pink underneath. They are sometimes edged with a black line around the dorsal, caudal and anal fins. A pretty fish even covered with slime. They are caught around coastal rocky reefs and feed on small fish, crustaceans and small invertebrates. The opalescent white flesh smokes brilliantly, brining firms it up tremendously. The possession limit is 30 fish.

This fish is suitable for all fish recipes in the book.

THAI FISH SOUP

A recipe suitable for most fishes caught around Bruny Island. It is more than a soup and can be eaten as a meal.

1 litre packet of fish stock

1 teaspoon chilli, crushed

2 teaspoons grated ginger

2 teaspoons garlic, crushed

1 tablespoon fish sauce

Juice and grated rind of one lime

2 cups coconut milk

200g noodles soaked in hot water for 15 minutes

600g cod fillet cut into bite sized pieces

12 mussels

200g baby spinach leaves

2 tablespoons chopped coriander

Empty contents of fish stock into a large saucepan and add the chilli, ginger, garlic, fish sauce and lime. Bring to the boil and simmer gently for ten minutes. Add the coconut milk, noodles, fish pieces and mussels, bring to the boil again, add the spinach leaves and chopped coriander. Serves four.

AUSTRALIAN SALMON

Australian Salmon or Black Back Salmon (*Arripis trutta*)

We had just finished talking to Nick Haddow at the cheese factory when Richard's phone rang. It was his fishing mate, John, ringing from Cloudy Bay to say that the water was jumping with Australian salmon. Having spent the early morning out on the oyster lease and then a few more hours photographing the cheeses, it was mid day. The sun was shining brilliantly from a cloudless sky, so we shot off down to Cloudy Bay Lagoon to catch a fish. There was a small industry here some years ago which saw 35 tons of small, white, sea shells taken into Hobart each week to be used in glass manufacture. Now the area is home to many rare species of birds that nest in the sand dunes above the high tide line. It has been made a nature reserve and peace and tranquillity reign.

John's beautiful house is literally on the edge of the lagoon and he seems to live in a permanent state of anticipation for catching the "Monarch". Shorts on, shoes off, bait in the fridge, fishing rod keenly leaning against the wall and the 'tinny' bobbing in the shallows, just a hop, skip and jump away from the living room.

This fish is sometimes called a cocky salmon and if allowed, will grow to four kilograms. It's an attractive torpedo-shaped fish of a silvery colour with brown spots, its pectoral fins are yellow. It is a feisty fish and once it is hooked, it runs and jumps repeatedly and fights hard. The flesh of the fish improves dramatically if the fish is bled immediately after it is caught.

We motored over to the far side of the blue lagoon; a shallow body of crystal clear water some 570 hectares when filled by the tide. The water was flowing out of the marine inlet when we arrived and it was here, in the deep channels that the salmon lurked. They were no longer jumping and were not easy to catch, but the fisher won. The size limit is 20 centimetres and possession limit is 15 fish.

I have suggested the curry recipe to balance the fishy flavour of the fillets.

AUSTRALIAN SALMON WITH CURRY AND BANANA

600g skinned, black back salmon fillets

1 tablespoon curry powder (I use Bolsts Hot)

1 tablespoon castor sugar

50g butter

Juice of 1 lime

2 tablespoons sour cream

1 banana

Salt to taste

Serve with rice

Mix the dry curry and sugar together on a plate. Dust the fish fillets with the curry mix, using it all.

Melt the butter in a frying pan and when bubbling add the fish fillets. Cook lightly until the sugar begins to caramelize turning the fish a golden brown. Squeeze the lime juice over the fish and lift from the pan – keep warm. Add the cream to the pan. Using a wooden spoon scrape all the 'bits' into the sauce. Cook until it begins to thicken and add the sliced banana. When warm serve sauce over the fish fillets with the cooked rice. Serves four.

Cloudy Bay

TRUMPETER

Bastard Trumpeter also called **Moki** or **Silver Trumpeter** *(Latridopsis forsteri)*

Trumpeter is most commonly caught in gill nets around Bruny Island's coastal reefs, although patient anglers will occasionally achieve more pleasure by catching one on rod, or even a line. They are quite hard to find in non-protected areas and are susceptible to over-fishing. They are very common in marine reserves; this suggests that reserve areas are effective for some fish species.

Bastard Trumpeter are a very handsome fish and have a dark grey-blue, slender body with longitudinal, golden stripes. The underbelly is of the palest silver. As they mature, they go out to deeper water and here they can grow up to four kilograms in weight.

The larger fish are often mistaken for that famed game fish the striped trumpeter *(Latris lineate)*. This fish, not related, is caught in much deeper water and can weigh in at 18 kilograms. It is an amazing fish that fights like hell. It is said to have the most prized eating flesh in Australia, indeed, some say the world. It's a very exciting ride to hook one of these.

The whole, baked, bastard trumpeter recipe is so well suited for this fish. The white flesh just peels off the bone. It is very succulent. We really enjoyed baking it whole. It was easy and looked most appealing. The fillets from this fish smoke well also.

The possession limit is ten fish and the minimum size limit 380 millimetres.

WHOLE BAKED TRUMPETER WITH PROVENÇAL SAUCE

1.5 kg trumpeter, gutted

5 lemon slices

5 bay leaves

5 large potatoes, peeled and sliced

2 tablespoons olive oil

Wash, clean and dry the trumpeter. Make five slashes diagonally across the top of the fish and insert a lemon slice and bay leaf into each slit. Put the oil in a baking dish large enough to hold the fish. Cover the base of the pan with sliced potatoes. Turn them in the oil. Place the fish on top of the potatoes. Sprinkle with a little salt and ground black pepper. Bake for 20 minutes at 180°C.

PROVENÇAL SAUCE

2 tablespoons olive oil

1 large onion, peeled

4 cloves garlic, crushed

4 large tomatoes, diced

1 small yellow capsicum, diced

1 small red capsicum, diced

1 teaspoon chopped oregano

Salt and pepper

2 tablespoons chopped parsley

Pour the olive oil into a saucepan and cook the onion and garlic very gently for five minutes without colouring. Add the tomato, capsicum and oregano and stew, with a lid on the saucepan, for ten minutes. Stir occasionally. Taste and add salt and pepper. Serve the baked fish with the Provençal sauce. Scatter with parsley.

SAMPHIRE

Samphire or Sea Asparagus *(tecticornia)*

Recently, samphire, a succulent coastal plant that thrives in saline environments has begun to appear on the menus of super-cool Australian restaurants as a trendy vegetable. It has in fact been eaten for centuries by those who live by the sea and are familiar with the plant. It has quite a history. Both the Greeks and Romans used it as a salad or steamed. It was collected extensively in Elizabethan times and used, amongst other things, to make a rather recherché green sauce, boiled, puréed and mixed with butter. It has been nibbled in East Anglia for centuries as pub grub and can occasionally be found served as a crunchy bar snack, preserved with spicy pickling vinegar.

The name samphire is a derivation of St. Pierre, who was the patron saint of fishermen. It is also known by the French as "sampiere" or "herbe de Saint-Pierre". Over time its leaves have shrunk to scales so that it looks green and bulbous giving it another name – "sea asparagus".

The herbalist Culpeper describes it as "a safe herb, very pleasant both in taste and stomach, helps digestion, and in some sort of opening obstructions of the liver and spleen".

Mythology tells of fishermen having been wrecked on barren coasts surviving many months by eating samphire, a boring but vitamin C filled diet.

In Australia, samphire is a different species from its European cousin, however, it still has the same qualities and was used by the early settlers in glass and soap production. Samphire was dried and burnt to an ash. The dried ash and a lot of salt was heated with sand on the beach and fused into a crude glass. This lent the name "glasswort" to its ever growing list of names. Soap makers used the ash which was evaporated into crystals of sodium hydroxide and heated with animal fats to produce coarse soaps hence it was sometimes called "soapwort". It has as many names as it has uses. As a small child I can recall going to the fishmongers with my mother to buy the weekly cod. The boater-hatted fishmonger would always put a handful of samphire in with the cutlets as he wrapped them in newspaper. When the cod was cooked, it was accompanied by a white sauce heavily laced with blanched samphire. Such was English cuisine in the 1960's.

Samphire can be seen in many coastal stretches on Bruny Island growing in the cracks of rocks. It is at its best for eating in December and January. It should be well washed before eating. It is crisp and salty and it is beautiful with fish and egg dishes.

QUINOA AND SAMPHIRE SALAD

Jill's recipe – quinoa *(Chenopodium)* is a relatively little known grain. Native to South America – the Incas called it "the mother of all grain". It is now grown in northern Tasmania. It is one of the super foods that is purported to have a higher protein content than meat, is low GI and gluten free. It is a good substitute for cous cous and rice. I have used it in the following recipe – it has a very nutty flavour but must be well washed under running water to get rid of any bitterness.

1 cup quinoa

2 cups water

100g marsh samphire

1 tablespoon of olive oil

Juice of one lemon

1 medium red onion, chopped

3 cloves garlic, crushed

2 tablespoons finely chopped preserved lemon

½ teaspoon smoked paprika

2 tablespoons chopped parsley

Wash the quinoa under running water and place in a saucepan with double the quantity of water. Bring to the boil and then simmer with a lid on the pot for ten minutes or until the water is absorbed. Spread on a plate to cool. Add the well-washed samphire to a pot of boiling water to blanch for five minutes. Drain and cool. Mix all other ingredients in a bowl. When well mixed pour it over the quinoa and samphire. Serve as a salad or with grilled fish.

SCRAMBLED EGGS WITH SMOKED SALMON AND SAMPHIRE TOASTS

5 slices stale bread

2 tablespoons olive oil

20g butter, for toasts

30g butter, for eggs

3 large free-range eggs

2 slices smoked salmon, very thinly shredded

½ cup marsh samphire, blanched and chopped small (asparagus can be used)

Heat oven to 180°C. I often make these toasties when the oven is warm after other baking. They keep well for a few days in a lidded container. Cut the crusts from five slices of stale bread and cut each slice into four squares about four centimetres each. Melt the butter and mix with oil and pour onto a baking tray. Coat both sides of the bread and bake until golden brown – about six minutes. Cool.

To make the scrambled eggs, whisk three large free-range eggs and season with salt and pepper. Using a non-stick pot, melt butter and add the eggs. Using a wooden spoon, stir gently and continuously. The eggs are cooked when they start to coagulate, making creamy curds. Now stir in the samphire and half of the shredded smoked salmon. Cook a little longer until the right, thick and creamy consistency is reached. Spoon on to the toasts and garnish each piece with a little shredded smoked salmon. Makes twenty toasts.

FLOUNDER

"Come on and eat. You can't fish and not eat". The Old Man and the Sea by Ernest Hemmingway

Tasmanian Flounder also called Greenback, Southern Flounder or Long Snout
(Rhombosolea tapirina)

Flounder can be caught at night using spears and lights. They have a green-grey upper side and a white under belly. They are able to camouflage themselves and can change colour to blend in with their environment. This makes them quite tricky to locate. They congregate in sandy bays, in shallow water, where they fossick on the sandy bottom for worms and small crustaceans. When we needed a flounder photograph for the book it seemed like a good opportunity for Richard to go on one of his 'great adventures'.

Four men took off in Richard's boat to catch and photograph flounder. His boat, the *Good Intent* has quite a story. It started out as a lifeboat built in Middlesex, England and is constructed from riveted aluminium plates. It was the lifeboat of the ill-fated *Lake Illawarra* that collided with Hobart's Tasman Bridge in 1975. The collision resulted in a span of the bridge falling on top of the ship sinking her to the muddy depths of the Derwent River. The few lucky crew who survived did so in their trusty lifeboat.

This very lifeboat is now retired and owned by Richard and Sue, always standing by for one of his fishing adventures. She is now named after a trading barge owned by one of his ancestors. The original *Good Intent* was built in 1877 by John Wilson at Port Cygnet, Southern Tasmania. At that time it was said to be "the handsomest barge on the Derwent".

True to his word Richard caught a good feed of flounder. Unfortunately none were bought back to me; they were all cooked in butter, over a camp fire, which is probably the very best way to eat them. At least they remembered to take a photograph first before they were devoured.

There is a minimum size limit of 25 centimetres (they can grow to about 40 centimetres) and a possession limit of 30 fish.

Butler's Beach

Labillardière Peninsula

Quiet Corner, Partridge Island

D'Entrecasteaux Channel

SCALLOPS

Commercial or **Southern Scallop** *(Pecten fumatus)*

The bivalve scallop shell is one of the most collected shells from our beaches. Who hasn't got one somewhere in their house or garden, picked up on a walk and taken home, because of its beauty? The perfect, radiating, fluted shell resembles a setting sun. It has become an emblem of fertility and protection. Paintings of Venus, especially that most famous, by Botticelli, depict this goddess of love and fertility rising from the sea on a scallop shell.

Tasmania once had a reputation for producing delicious, sweet and tender scallops in great quantity and excellent value. Southern Tasmanian scallops have been the main species targeted and caught by various methods for well over a hundred years. Catches were at their maximum in the late 1960's when the annual Tasmanian harvest peaked at 13,000 tonnes. Due to greed and a careless attitude to fishing methods the scallop beds were absolutely devastated. It has been estimated that dredges with steel fingers, used in the Channel, killed as many scallops as were caught. Inevitably the fishery died. This goes to show how important it is that fisheries are well managed and if not, they can go terribly wrong.

The D'Entrecasteaux Channel has for many years been open only to recreational divers, with strict size and bag limits. Here, there is a species called "the doughboy" *(Chlamys asperrimus)*. These small, round, sponge encrusted scallops, once in great quantity, would provide fabulous feasts for keen divers. Alas no more.

The scallop beds are now carefully monitored each year and the Minister for Fisheries makes a final decision as to whether the areas should remain closed or have a short trial season. It is based on information provided by scientists from government departments, TAFI (Tasmanian Aquaculture and Fisheries Institute) and DPIPWE (Department of Primary Industries, Parks, Water and Environment). One of the greater problems that the fishery poses is the sporadic recruitment of the species and how researchers can ensure future recruitment successes. This year the Minister announced – "The D'Entrecasteaux Channel is closed for the 2012 season. The area closure was necessary to protect scallop stocks and reduce the likelihood of long term closures".

This causes much angst and speculation by the recreational divers who have their own theories about starfish eating the scallops and that, because of the "closed area" regulations, scallops are left in their beds to die from old age. In any event it is a very sad story and serves only to remind us of the fragility of our fisheries.

CEVICHE OF SCALLOPS

This is an entrée scallop recipe in which the scallop is not actually cooked with heat. The acid in the lime juice will coagulate, or 'set', the protein. It has the same effect as cooking. This method of preparing seafood comes from South America. It is light to eat and utterly delicious. Cubes of raw fish can be added to the marinade to make the scallops go further.

500g fresh scallops, sliced horizontally into thin slices

Juice and shredded zest of four limes, keeping the zest for end

½ small red onion finely chopped

1 red chilli, de-seeded and finely chopped

1 clove garlic, finely minced

2 tablespoons chopped coriander

3 tomatoes seeded, skinned and chopped

1 tablespoon olive oil

Place scallops, lime juice, onion, chilli and garlic into a ceramic or plastic bowl. Cover and marinate for at least two hours, turning occasionally. When ready, strain off liquid. Add coriander, tomatoes and olive oil. Serve in small bowls with the zest scattered over the top.

How fortunate we have been to have experienced the magnificence of a sweet Tasmanian scallop.

It is the traditional emblem of St. James. Thousands of representations can be found carved into buildings on the routes the pilgrims walked, "el camino de Santiago", converging at St. James' shrine in Santiago, North Western Spain. Those who have made this gruelling walk bring a special scallop shell back into their homes as a keepsake.
There is one over the door in Richard and Sue's bothy, brought back after a pilgrimage to Santiago in 2011.

ATLANTIC SALMON

Atlantic Salmon (*Salmo salar*)

In 1982, a pioneer of Norwegian salmon farming visited Tasmania and declared it to be an ideal place for Atlantic salmon culture. He was right, as it has grown into a considerable business with about 32,000 tonnes of salmon produced each year worth $350 million. This is a fantastic boost to the Tasmanian economy.

Most of the farms are concentrated in the D'Entrecasteaux Channel and the Huon River. You will see one farm as the ferry docks at Bruny Island, to the north-east of the terminal. There are rings and circles visible on top of the water, but most of the business is under the water. Nearly eighty five per cent of the Tasmania's Atlantic salmon produce is sold on the mainland (only seven per cent is sold overseas) and there's every chance that the Atlantic salmon you will buy from the supermarket, will be Tasmanian.

Tasmania boasts a pest and disease free status and the cleanest water and best climate in the world for growing salmon. The spectacular growth of this industry has, however, inadvertently spawned a recreational fishery. There is no such fish as a wild Atlantic salmon in Australia. Occasionally there will be a break-out of salmon from a net that has been savaged by a shark, dolphin or a seal. The escapees become game for anyone who finds and catches them. The word goes out among the recreational fishers and tinnies can be seen scouring the waters. Searching for the bow-wave of a large salmon is made easier with the use of Polaroid sunglasses. The development of stronger nets outside the softer inner nets makes break-outs almost a thing of the past. This is bad luck on the fishers but good luck for the fishmongers.

Bish is a smoke house, restaurant bar very close to the Bruny ferry terminal where the chef Tony McLaine hot smokes local salmon in a neat functional smoker. He sources fresh local Atlantic salmon, hot smokes it, to be eaten in the restaurant. It can also be bought from his pantry and is one of the best ways of eating this fish that I know. He also smokes the local wallaby which, when thinly sliced makes a most unusual and delicious addition to salads, sandwiches and risottos.

Here is a very quick and easy recipe that uses hot smoked Atlantic salmon. It is an appetizing starter or light main course.

HOT SMOKED SALMON SALAD WITH NOODLES

Dressing

2 tablespoons lime juice

2 tablespoons soy sauce

2 tablespoons olive oil

1 tablespoon fish sauce

1 teaspoon sesame oil

1 teaspoon sambal olek

1 tablespoon grated ginger

Salad

250g hot smoked salmon

300g fresh udon noodles

1 bunch spring onions

To make the dressing put all the ingredients into a screw top jar. Shake and allow to stand for five minutes.

Cook the noodles in boiling salted water. Strain and tip onto a plate to cool. Cut the salmon into three centimetre slices and flake into the cooled noodles. Cut the white ends of the onions into thin slices and add to the noodles. Pour over the dressing and garnish with chopped spring onion greens. A light lunch for four.

SEA RUN TROUT

Sea Run Trout *(Salmo trutta)*

These are brown trout, originally introduced from England in 1864, as a sport fish for the emerging Tasmanian gentry. It was, after several false starts, a most successful immigration – the river and lake trout fishery has become internationally renowned.

But not every brown trout stays in the river to be stalked by fervent, fresh water fishers. There are those who spend their first two to three years in fresh water. As they grow they are enticed to the nutrient enriched coastal areas, where they spend one to two seasons, before returning to their river. In salt water their appearance changes and they become predominately silver, sleeker and bullet-like in shape, adapting to a life in the ocean. Because of this new life at sea, chasing small fish and dealing with the often rough conditions, they have very high levels of physical fitness. They are firm and if their diet has included crustaceans their flesh will be quite deep orange. Their flavour will be infinitely superior to any farmed salmonoid you can buy.

Caught at sea, they are usually around three kilograms, but giants have been known. In the late 1800's Governor Hamilton was recorded as having caught a 13 kilogram trout. They are usually caught from shore by serious fishers, who use an array of spinners, flies and endless hours of patience. The more humble fisher may be lucky enough to catch one as he fishes from his tinny out in the estuarine waters of the Huon River. They are the holy grail of Channel fish.

Farmed trout are produced commercially in Tasmania's pure waters. It is a great product with a superior flesh and taste to the farmed Atlantic salmon, but doesn't rate with wild caught fish.

GRAVLAX CURED WITH A BEETROOT, VODKA AND HERB TOPPING

500g skin on sea run trout fillet, scaled

Marinade

5 tablespoons coarse salt

3 tablespoons raw sugar

200g fresh beetroot, peeled and finely grated

Zest of one lemon grated

4 tablespoons vodka

1 tablespoon each of finely chopped basil, chervil, chives, dill and parsley

Horseradish Sauce

6 tablespoons crème fraîche

4 tablespoons grated horseradish

1 tablespoon castor sugar

Juice of half a lemon

1 tablespoon chopped chives

Salt and pepper to taste

Mix marinade ingredients together.

To prepare the fillet remove any pin bones. There is a wonderful pair of Japanese, blunt tweezers on the market that will do this. Put the fillet face down, on a cling film covered tray and with a very sharp knife cut three or four slits across the skin side of the fillet. Turn the fillet over – flesh side up.

Mix all the other ingredients together and press the mixture over the flesh, covering it. Wrap the cling film over the top of the trout. Put another tray on top of the fillet and weigh down with heavy weights. Chill for at least 24 hours by which time the trout will be infused with a fresh earthy, herby flavour and cured with the salt and vodka. Clean off the herbs and beetroot with kitchen paper and your fish is ready for slicing. Mix horseradish sauce ingredients and serve with red onions, capers and slices of Peter Barefoot's very easy bread (recipe on page 20). Serves six as an entrée.

CRAYFISH

Southern Rock Lobster or Crayfish (*Jasus edwardsii*)

There are a few old fishers around who remember when the price of crayfish was measured by the "score", so that ten shillings could buy you twenty crays. Today there is a global price for crayfish set by our export market. This, and the costs incurred by the fishermen for catching the fish, has escalated to a point at which the eating of lobster is a luxury only for the very rich. Australian lobster fishing must be one of the most over-regulated fisheries in the world. Luckily, this is not so for the recreational fisher.

Anyone over the age of ten can buy a licence for one pot and then proceed to catch a daily bag limit of three or five crayfish (depending where they are caught) for the entire crayfish season. This of course is not quite as wonderful as it sounds, since amateur fishers are not allowed to sell any of their catch, and even the sublime flavour and texture of the Southern Rock Lobster will pall if one eats too many. Believe me – I know. When George and I were lobster fishing off the West Australian Coast back in the seventies, crayfish was our main protein source. We were desperately trying to make the bank payments for our first boat and our diet consisted mostly of our catch, crayfish, in scrambled eggs for brekkie, in sandwiches for lunch and salads or grilled at night. Oh yes! You can eat too much of anything – even crayfish. The only time I eat crayfish now is when my grandchildren catch them. I just love it when they arrive home from a Bruny Island fishing trip salt encrusted, hair awry and bursting with good health and happiness and hand a lively lobster to their grandmother.

The rules and regulations regarding recreational rock lobster fishing are strict, intricate and ever changing. Once again, I urge you to thoroughly read the Recreational Sea Fishing Guide that is renewed at the end of October every year.

In my mind, the only way to eat crayfish is boiled in seawater and eaten warm, dipped in home-made mayonnaise. I will put this essential recipe for mayonnaise here. It can be used as the basis for so many sauces.

MAYONNAISE

2 large egg yolks

1 teaspoon hot English mustard

1 teaspoon cider vinegar

1 teaspoon lemon juice

Salt and freshly ground black pepper, to taste

500 ml good quality peanut or olive oil, I often use a mixture of both

All the ingredients must be at room temperature. Using a plastic or ceramic bowl, whisk all the ingredients together, except the oil. Add the oil in a thin stream whisking vigorously, until it is all incorporated. A blender or food processor will do this equally well. Warm water can be added if the mixture is too thick.

CRAYFISH RAVIOLI

This is another case of the feeding of the five thousand – or – how to make a delicious morsel go a long way. This is an involved recipe but gives great satisfaction. Sauce aurora is a classic French sauce but I have renamed it Sauce Southern Lights to make it more local.

Ravioli pasta

400g plain flour

1 teaspoon salt

4 eggs

2 tablespoons olive oil

1 egg white for egg wash (keep yolk for filling)

Combine all ingredients in a food processor until the dough begins to cling together. Then put it on to a floured surface and knead for a few minutes, until a firm ball is formed. Wrap in cling film and put in a cool place to rest for an hour or so.

Cut the dough in half and using a floured surface, feed it through a pasta machine at the thickest setting. Keeping the pasta well floured and again put it through the next setting. Repeat the process until the pasta sheet has been through the machine enough times to get it to its thinnest. Repeat with the other piece of dough.

You will now have two sheets of pasta the same width as your pasta machine (about 15 centimetres) wide and quite long. Cut each sheet into three long strips giving you six pieces. Brush the surface of three strips with egg white. Place teaspoons full of filling five centimetres apart down the centre of each of the three strips. Cover each filled strip with a second strip of dough. Using your fingers, seal the two strips together around the sides and between the filling. You can now cut out your ravioli by either using a cookie cutter (about 5 centimetres in diameter) or use a fluted edged pastry wheel. I have a fabulous little toy called a 'pastabike' that children love to use if they are helping. It is run over the pastry and can cut between the ravioli with great ease. You should now have between 25 and 30 raviolis ready to cook.

Bring a large pan of salted water to the boil. Reduce to a simmer and drop in the ravioli a few at a time. As soon as they float, lift them out with a slotted spoon and keep them warm until they are all cooked. Serve covered with Sauce Southern Lights.

Crayfish filling

400g cooked crayfish meat (ten whole green prawns could be used instead)

1 small red chilli very finely chopped

1 tablespoon of chopped parsley

1 egg yolk, keep the egg white for the egg wash

Pinch cayenne

Place all ingredients for filling into a food processor and blitz until they amalgamate. Put in a bowl in the fridge until ready to use.

Sauce Southern Lights

5 tablespoons butter

2 cloves garlic, minced

1 can cherry tomatoes

½ cup vodka

¼ cup chopped parsley

¾ cup heavy cream

Melt the butter in a saucepan and add the minced garlic. Cook for a minute until the garlic is transparent but not coloured. Add the tomatoes and vodka and simmer for five minutes. When ready to use, bring to the boil and add the parsley and cream. Warm but do not re-boil. Pour over the cooked ravioli.
An entrée for four.

FREE-RANGE CHOOKS

"The bird that gives birth every day". An old Egyptian saying

"Be patient for in time even an egg will walk". Quote from a fortune cookie

Chicken (*Gallus gallus domesticus*) – a subspecies of the **Red Jungle Fowl (*Gallus gallus*)**

Over 50 billion chickens are reared world-wide each year as a food source. A good two thirds of these are raised by intensive farming methods, but the remainder are 'free-range'. This story is about those free-range or "happy hens".

Keeping hens in your backyard or garden was pretty common before the 1950's but with the shift to urbanised living, the urgency to work so hard and have so little time for ourselves, the home grown hens lost favour. However, the wheel turns and once again a greener life-style and self-sufficiency have become de rigueur.

The joy of keeping hens is something of a well kept secret. There are so many pluses; they can be kept in a small area; they need little attention and are not expensive to feed; they keep pest insects at bay in your garden as they scratch and turn the soil. Chicken manure and old straw will make a brilliant fertiliser, particularly around citrus trees and rose bushes. Free-range eggs taste much better than bought eggs; they have a much richer colour and add a tremendous lift to your cooking – and you know how old they are. Then there is the financial side – you can actually make money from selling your surplus eggs.

Hens make wonderful pets and can teach your children about caring for and looking after animals; the simple joy that they show when they find a warm, brown egg in the nest is just beautiful. They learn too that eggs are laid by hens and do not come in cardboard boxes from the supermarket.

By now you can tell I am pretty keen on chooks. I have always kept enough hens to supply my family with fresh eggs and now that I am retired I have time to slow down and watch my chooks go about their busy lives. I find their 'pecking order' very entertaining. Gallus, my rooster, is quite the gentleman and stands back to let his girls rush past him out of the house. He will always let them eat first, often presenting morsels to his favourite girl. She, of course, comes at the top of the pecking order, sleeping next to him on the roost at night. The rest have to jostle for a place, the lowest often sleeping on the ground below.

I have a very good neighbour, Helen, who has been helping me edit this book. She is frightened of my hens and cannot visit me unless they are locked up in their run. Her fear is so real that she is unable to eat eggs or chicken meat and won't even sit on a cushion embroidered with a hen. She has a very real phobia called "Alektorophobia". Fortunately, most Bruny Islanders are free from this state and nearly all the homes and properties that I visited were alive with healthy chooks and bantams scratching around their yards in search of insects.

Sal and Trevor who live at Sheepwash Bay are typical new-age people with a wonderful flock of fine, healthy, ISA Brown hens. This breed of hen is the absolute top layer, being a hybrid of the Rhode Island Red crossed with the Rhode Island White and developed in France in the 1970's. The ISA part of the name stands for Institut de Sélection Animale and she is bred for her temperament. She is friendly, pretty, docile, good with children, and she lays prodigiously – more than 300 eggs in her first year and she doesn't go broody. She is a sweet bird that will keep on and on supplying you with eggs.

If you have owned laying hens for several years, given them names and they have become your friends, it can be very hard to despatch them when they no longer lay eggs. Hilary has one remaining chook from a flock she had years ago. The rest have all dropped off the perch, as it were. Ruth, the chook, spends her retirement eating bugs in Hilary Cane's stunning garden.

SARAH'S MANDARIN BRIOCHE CHOCOLATE PUDDING

My daughter Sarah is the queen of desserts. She is continually striving to come up with new and delicious pudding recipes for Mures Upper Deck restaurant. She and her husband Rick have owned and run the seafood restaurant in Hobart for nearly twenty years now. This desert served with a mandarin semi freddo ice cream is new, self indulgent and utterly scrumptious. It is quite a time consuming recipe, but if taken slowly, step-by-step, will give the maker a great deal of satisfaction. It is "Oh so delicious".

Mandarin curd

225g castor sugar

Grated zest and juice of 2 mandarins

3 eggs

110g unsalted butter, cut into small pieces

Whisk the sugar, zest, juice of mandarins and three eggs together in a saucepan. Place over a medium heat and slowly whisk in the butter pieces making sure all the butter melts. Keep whisking over a low heat until the curd thickens. Do not boil or you will have mandarin scrambled eggs. Chill in fridge.

Hilary Cane's garden

Mandarin curd semi freddo

4 eggs, separated

2 x ½ cups sugar

500 ml cream

1 cup of the mandarin curd

Cream together four egg yolks and half a cup of sugar. Whisk egg whites to stiff peaks. Slowly whisk in half a cup of sugar. Whip cream to soft peaks and fold in the egg yolk mixture and one cup of the chilled mandarin curd. Lastly fold in the egg whites. Freeze overnight. Take out of fridge ten minutes before eating to soften slightly.

Brioche chocolate pudding

6 thick slices of a brioche loaf, buttered, crusts removed and cut into 3 cm cubes

150g bitter chocolate, chopped

400 ml pouring cream

400 ml full cream milk

1 split vanilla pod

5 large eggs

300g sugar

Zest from one mandarin

Icing sugar to decorate

Butter six 250 millilitre soufflé dishes or one large one and a half litre soufflé dish. Half fill each ramekin dish with bread cubes. Evenly sprinkle the chocolate over the bread and then top up with the rest of the bread. Make sure that the top cubes are butter side up. Bring pouring cream, milk, vanilla pod and mandarin zest to the boil. Cream together eggs and sugar. Remove the vanilla pod and add scalded milk to the egg and sugar mix, whisking well. Pour this mixture into the soufflé dishes over the bread and chocolate. Keep refilling and pushing the top bits down as brioche soaks up the mixture. Place a folded tea-towel in the bottom of a baking dish and stand the six soufflé dishes on it. Pour boiling water into the baking dish so that it comes half way up the soufflé dishes. Cook at 170°C. for 30 minutes until puffed golden and set. Dust with icing sugar and serve with a large scoop of semi freddo. Serves 6.

SAL'S SOUP

When Trevor's chooks have finally stopped laying he prepares them for Sal to use in the kitchen. Free-range chickens are a totally different beast from the bought ones. They do need more cooking but the flavour is pure chook. Here is Sal's wholesome, warm recipe.

For the stock

I home grown chook

2 brown onions, peeled

Salt and pepper

For the soup

3 tablespoons of butter

2 carrots, peeled

½ sweet potato

½ swede

3 sticks celery

250g pumpkin

¼ head broccoli

¼ head cauliflower

1 packet cream of chicken soup

Put the chook and sliced onions into a large stock pot and cover with water and season with salt and white pepper. Bring to the boil and then simmer for one hour. Strain the stock from the chicken and allow to settle, and cool, so that the fat can be skimmed off the top. Pull the chicken apart into smallish pieces. Discard the bones.

Cut the carrots, potatoes, swede, celery and pumpkin into small slices. Melt the butter in the large pot and part cook the vegetables over a very low heat for ten minutes. Do not brown. Add the stock and chook pieces. Bring to the boil and then simmer very gently for 30 minutes. At the end of this time put in the sliced broccoli and cauliflower. Mix the packet soup in bowl with 100 millilitres cold water. Pour the mix into your soup and cook for a further 15 minutes. Taste for additional salt and pepper if needed.

PORK

"I sometimes wonder how the flavour of our run of the mill Sunday roasts might benefit from a touch of a Sage". Jinasiri Bhikkhu (aka Jason Chan)

Bruny Island Foods

Pig Heaven is situated half way down South Bruny Island near Lunawanna, in the foothills of Mt. Mangana. We visited Ross O'Meara and his pigs on a cold, wet, grey day, but this is the weather that pigs love. The teenagers and little baby piglets, covered in mud, were behaving like delinquent children, racing around, splashing into mud ponds and jostling to get close to Ross for a pat and scratch behind the ears. The enormously large boars and sows waited for Ross's attention with the patience of the elderly. Pleasurable grunting noises could be heard coming from these happy pigs, a little like the noise a dog will make when you scratch that special spot. What a wonderful environment for these lucky creatures!

Ross produces two varieties of rare pig, the rarest being "Donna", his Wessex Saddleback sow. This large black pig, with a white saddle-like band around its middle is renowned for its fine flesh. It originally roamed the New Forest in England foraging for acorns and rooting for clover. Unfortunately they couldn't adapt to intensive farming methods and so became extinct in Great Britain. As luck would have it, breeding pigs had been sent out to Australia and New Zealand where the Wessex Saddleback is now established, but in a much diminished way. They are very large pigs and are grown essentially for bacon and hams. A green leg ham can weigh up to seven kilograms. It is brined and then smoked in a wood smoker. This old fashioned leg ham is perfect to cook for Christmas. Ross makes the occasional Prosciutto by the time-honoured method of slow air drying, but this is for family and friends only and is not commercial.

The Berkshire Pig is another vulnerable rare breed facing extinction. This black pig is a great character and will be recognised by most as "Pig Wig" in "The Tale of Pigling Bland" by Beatrix Potter, and the antagonist pig in "Animal Farm". The Japanese have taken these pigs to their hearts and stomachs and are rearing them as Kagoshima Kurobuta, which literally translates as "Black Hog of Kagoshima". It is known as the Wagyu of the pork world, famous for its exceptionally tender, marbled meat and sweet and juicy taste. It is also firmer and darker than supermarket pork, with much more flavour.

Ross has discovered a niche market by producing higher quality meat that can be sold directly to consumers and chefs. They know what they are buying and are prepared to pay a little more for it.

Pork produced by Ross can be bought at The Farmers Market held every Sunday at the Melville Street Car Park and at the Common Ground Store in Salamanca Place.

Donna

PORK RILLETTES

Jill's recipe – pork rillettes are a fabulous standby to have in your fridge – great for lunch or as an appetizer. If you don't have time to make them yourself Ross makes them and sells them at the Farmers Market.

1 kg skinned and boned belly of pork

3 cloves garlic, peeled

10 juniper berries

1 teaspoon black peppercorns

1 teaspoon dried mace

2 sprigs fresh thyme

150 ml white wine

Heat oven to 140°C. Skin and bone the pork and place in a ceramic baking dish. Sprinkle with the herbs and spices and pour over the wine. Cover with a lid or foil and bake for three hours, or until the meat is completely tender. Take out the meat and strain the fat and juices, discarding the 'bits'. The garlic will have dissolved into the juices. Pull the meat and fat apart using two forks and taste for seasoning before packing into ceramic or glass pots. Pour over the juice and fat and make sure there are no air pockets in the jar and that there is a layer of fat covering the meat. This will keep for at least a week in the refrigerator.

Spread on crusty bread with pickles or chutney. I have served it here with the pickled cherries (recipe on page 20).

SLOW ROASTED SHOULDER OF PORK

This recipe of Ross's is an old fashioned, slow-cooked, heart warmer. It is a great dish for a small or large number of people. The anchovies might sound a bit much but once cooked they add a fantastic, natural, salty flavour and depth to this roast. Takes six and a half hours.

1 head of garlic, peeled

1 small handful of sage

1 tablespoon chopped fresh rosemary

1 tablespoon fennel seeds, ground

3 anchovy fillets

1 pinch of chilli flakes

3 shallots, peeled

1 tablespoon olive oil

Sea salt flakes

Ground black pepper

4 kg free-range pork shoulder, skin on and well scored

1 lemon

750 ml of white wine

Preheat the oven to 200°C. Place the garlic, sage, rosemary, fennel, anchovy, chilli, shallots, olive oil and seasoning into a mortar and pestle and grind to a paste. Rub the under-side of the pork shoulder being careful not to get any on the skin. Slice the lemons and place into a roasting tray large enough for the pork shoulder.

Place the pork shoulder into the roasting tray skin side up. Add the wine then cover the tray with a layer of foil making sure that it is completely sealed. Cook in the oven for one hour then reduce the temperature to 150°C. and cook for a further five and a half hours. Make sure you check and baste your pork every hour.

Remove the pork from the roasting tray and pour the juice into a saucepan. To crisp up the skin increase the oven temperature to 200°C. and replace the pork. This should only take 30 minutes at tops so keep an eye on the pork during this process because it will cook quickly.

Whilst the pork is finishing, reduce the cooking liquor by half, skimming the fat off as you go. When ready to serve just pour the liquor over the top. Serve with some fresh greens and root vegetables. Serves ten.

BEEF

"The mere brute pleasure of reading – the sort of pleasure a cow
must have in grazing". *Lord Chesterfield*

When I watch cattle feeding on verdant, green pasture I feel at peace with the world. There is a sense of ageless permanency, a reminder of times past. The road that meanders through Bruny Island reveals one beautiful pastoral scene after another. There are Herefords, Aberdeen Angus, Belted Galloways and Highland cattle on relatively small scale, boutique farms – all feeding from lush chemical-free pasture. The Highland cattle with their long horns and red, wavy, hairy coats must feel very much at home in the depth of Tasmania's winter. The high rainfall, strong winds and stress free conditions ensure that the island's beef is of the highest quality. The fact that they are "free from antibiotic and hormone growth promotants", like all Tasmanian beef, makes the meat much sought after.

Teresa and Ralph spend most weekends at Sheepwash Bay building their shack. They no longer live in the caravan while they work, it's nearly finished so that they can now sleep in a real bed and cook on a gas stove. But old habits die hard and the camp fire and Dutch oven have not been forgotten.

They fell in love with the island and its lifestyle when they came to the launch of "The Photographer the Cook and the Fisherman" the last book on which Richard, George and I collaborated. They immediately went out and bought a patch of Bruny Island to build on. Building makes you very hungry and without a kitchen one must improvise. Teresa brings a large beef pot roast over with her when she visits at week-ends. She very generously shares this with friends and neighbours and so the "pot roast Saturday night" evolved.

The pot roast comes from either the fore or hindquarter of the beast and has more fat than the finer cuts. This gives it much more flavour. It will need slower cooking to prevent it from toughening, because it is a much more exercised part of the animal. It is ideal for slow roasting in a camp oven over an open fire.

The camp oven has been in use since the early seventeen hundreds. Designed by the Dutch, they were first called Dutch ovens. Made from cast iron they last forever and only improve with age and use. This same Dutch oven was taken to South Africa and used by the Voortrekkers where it became known as a "potjie" or "little pot". Early French chefs would use similar vessels which soon evolved into "casseroles" and then the enamelled beautiful Le Creuset and Le Chasseur were developed. Once you have conquered the anomalies of using the coals of a camp fire you will find that it will open the door to a whole new world of campfire cooking. Bread, damper, vegetables and delicious stews can be cooked in this versatile pot and it makes the best Bruny bouillabaisse imaginable.

Our primitive senses are stimulated by the smell of wood smoke, the crackling of burning logs as a large piece of beef roasts in a pot on the open fire. The juices flow and food never tasted so good. Thank you Teresa and Ralph for your great hospitality and those good times around the fire.

BEEFSTEAK, MUSHROOM AND STOUT PIE

4 pie tins (3 cm deep and about 7 cm wide at the base)

500g topside steak, cut into 3 cm chunks

2 tablespoons plain flour, seasoned with salt and pepper

2 tablespoons olive oil

2 medium onions, cut in half and thinly sliced

4 cloves garlic, crushed

200g honey brown mushrooms, sliced

2 bay leaves, crushed

2 sprigs thyme

300 ml Cascade Stout

2 sheets puff pastry

1 small beaten egg for egg wash

Heat the oil in a heavy based saucepan that has a tight fitting lid. Put the steak in a bowl and coat with seasoned flour, put in to the hot oil and brown on all surfaces. Add the onions, garlic and mushrooms and cook for a few moments. Sprinkle in the herbs, add the stout and bring to the boil stirring gently. Turn the stove down to a gentle simmer. Cover tightly and slow stew for an hour. Take off lid and continue to cook until the meat is tender and most of the liquid has evaporated. Turn stewed beef into a bowl and cool completely.

Preheat oven to 180°C. Semi-thaw the sheets of puff pastry and using one sheet, line the four oiled tins. Spoon in the filling and brush the pastry edges with egg wash. Cut the remaining sheet of pastry into four and cover the four pies. Press down around the edges to seal. Decorate and brush with the remaining egg wash. Bake for thirty minutes or until golden brown. This recipe will make one large or four small pies.

TERESA'S POT ROAST

Probably one of the most important factors in this sort of cooking is to light the fire sufficiently early and have enough dry wood. You need to keep good red coals burning for at least one and a half hours. It is necessary to comply with fire restrictions and never to have an open fire in forest reserves.

1.5 to 2 kg beef roast

2 tablespoons olive oil

1 tablespoon pepper berries

Potatoes

Carrots

Parsnips

Pumpkin

Grind one tablespoonful pepper berries and massage with the oil into the beef. Leave overnight in the fridge. Prepare the vegetables by cutting into regular sizes and sprinkle with salt and pepper and a little oil. Wrap the meat and the vegetables separately in aluminium foil. Put a trivet in the base of your camp oven and place the meat and vegetables snugly inside. Put the oven on the red coals.

You may think that it is now time for that glass of red wine or beer – perhaps it is, but the pot and fire must be tended. The fire must not be allowed to go out, but by the same token it must not be too hot. As you will realise, this is not an exact science and it's a lot of fun experimenting. Check after an hour and if the vegetables are cooked they can be taken out of the oven and put on the lid to keep warm. The meat may take another half an hour or so to cook. The slower you cook the meat the more tender it will become. Serves four.

Court Island, Cape Bruny

WINE

"Good wine is a good familiar creature if it be well used".
William Shakespeare (1564-1616) Othello, II. iii. (315)

Bruny Island Premium Wines

The first grape vine was planted at Adventure Bay in 1778 by Captain William Bligh but it was not until the early 1960's that the great visionary, Claudio Alcorso, threw down the gauntlet. He declared that the wine growing conditions in Tasmania were akin to those in Burgundy and would produce great wines, and that the once-famous vineyards of Southern Australia would one day be compared with Algeria. This outlandish idea, that Tasmania could become a great wine growing region, was scoffed at by the North Island vintners. Claudio pioneered the Tasmanian wine industry at his winery, Morilla, and showed the world that he was not wrong.

There are now over a hundred vineyards in Tasmania and Bruny Island Premium Wines, at Wayeree Estate, Lunawanna, is Australia's most southerly vineyard. It was started in 1997.

It is here that Richard and Bernice Woolley, with the help of Bernice's father, John Dillon, have planted two hectares of vines on an ideal, north-westerly facing slope. Pinot Noir and Chardonnay grapes enjoy warm summers and long, sunny but cool autumn days. The slow ripening of the fruit adds to the flavour of the wine, as do the oak casks in which the wines are matured. The product is a medal-winning wine.

This is a family business and Bernice's forebears were some of the first settlers on the island, having arrived at Adventure Bay in 1878. The strong family ties become more obvious at pruning and picking when it's all hands to the pump. It seems that most of the islanders come to help pick too. It could have something to do with the feast that the Woolleys put on for their pickers once the grapes are harvested.

Wines are made on the premises by Richard and Bernice and it was Bernice's talented mother who painted the very distinctive labels on the wines.

The winery cellar door is open most days for tastings and sales, between 11 am and 4 pm. It is a most pleasant break in your drive around the island. Try the silver medal winning Chardonnay – it's a cracker!

MUSHROOM RISOTTO

Bernice's recipe – Bernice suggested a risotto recipe – and I think most of us like the idea of cooking with a glass of wine at hand. When I make this recipe for the vegetarian members of my family I use vegetable stock and withhold the bacon.

50g butter

100g smoky bacon, cut into fine strips

150g button mushrooms

150g honey brown mushrooms

1.5 litre chicken stock

250 ml white wine

1 medium size onion, finely chopped

4 cloves garlic, crushed

440g Arborio rice

Finely grated rind of 1 lemon

½ cup chopped parsley

70g grated Parmesan cheese

Melt half the butter (25 grams) in a large heavy based pan. Cook the bacon, stirring often for three minutes and then add mushrooms and cook until mushrooms soften for about six minutes. Transfer the mixture to a bowl. Put stock and wine into a saucepan and bring to boil then allow to simmer.

Melt remaining (25 grams) butter in the large pan, add the onions and garlic, cook gently without colouring then add the rice and stir for two minutes. Add the mushroom mixture. Add the simmering stock and wine, half a cupful at a time, stirring until absorbed. Continue to do this until all the liquid has been used. It will take about twenty minutes. The rice should be tender but quite wet.

Remove pan from the heat and stir in half the Parmesan cheese, the lemon rind and parsley. Season well with salt, freshly ground black pepper and sprinkle with remaining cheese.

PINOT NOIR FRUIT SOUP

Jill's recipe – this is an extravagantly delightful dessert for a hot summer evening. Light, bright and colourful, it is very different and visually appealing.

400 ml pinot noir

60g sugar

I cup blueberries

2 cups raspberries

2 cups strawberries – halve and quarter if they are too big

Mascarpone honey topping

140g mascarpone cheese

1 tablespoon runny honey

1 tablespoon milk

A handful mint sprigs

Heat the wine and sugar until the sugar dissolves – bring the mixture to the boil. Cool. When cool pour over the mixed berries either in one large glass bowl or four individual glasses.

Stir the honey into the mascarpone cheese and soften with the milk to a smooth coating consistency. Serve spooned over the fruit or on the side in a small bowl and dot with mint leaves.

© Jill Mure

This is the 12th book by Tasmanian landscape, yachting and food photographer Richard Bennett. It is the next chapter in a life in which he has constantly sought and found fresh inspiration to illustrate the island he holds so dear to his heart .

He is the doyen of photographers of Tasmania and Tasmanian life. The Tasmanian landscape is his still-life passion, ocean racing his action forte. Because of his love of food and cooking, a book on Tasmania's Bruny Island and it's quality produce was a natural subject for him.

Richard has photographed every Sydney-Hobart yacht race since 1974. His images are synonymous with the race itself.

In 1999 he won the Nikon-Kodak Australian Press Photographer of the Year Award for the best sports photograph with his images of the 1998 Sydney-Hobart yacht race tragedy. In 2003 he was awarded a Centenary Medal for his promotion of Tasmania through his photography. In 2006 he won the Photo Imaging Council of Australia's highest award, The Gold Tripod. He is a past national president, a Fellow and an Honorary Fellow of the Australian Institute of Professional Photography and is a past chairman of the Australian Professional Photography Awards.

He and his wife Sue live on Bruny Island.

There are few careers that stir the passions like cooking. It can be professionally competitive and brilliantly creative, pitting those at the top of the culinary pile to constantly source new ideas to shape our view of food. It's a long way to the top.

By any measure Jill Mure has made it. Her name is synonymous with fine fare, especially fine fish fare. Some would say there's briny in her blood.

Alfie Baker probably had something to do with Jill's love of food. Alfie was Jill's father who ran Britain's oldest and poshest seafood restaurant "Scott's" in Piccadilly, London. At a very early age Jill was tutored in the finer points of cooking fish.

No wonder she married a fisherman. The dashing George Mure took her to sea after they migrated to Australia in 1962 and together they fished for ten years from Fremantle in Western Australia to the Gulf of Carpentaria and Papua New Guinea.

It was a natural progression from this remarkable adventure to the establishment in 1974 of one of Tasmania's most famous restaurants unpretentiously called Mures Fish House in Battery Point. Jill cooked while George brought in the catch. The food was simple and sensational. In 1987 they took the bold step of moving to Victoria Dock expanding their fishery interests into Mures Fish Centre. Freshly-caught fish are landed right there from their boats to the doorstep.

George died in 2003 and Jill handed over the business to her children Will and Sarah.

With time on her hands she has continued sharing her wonderful culinary knowledge and love of the sea and its bounty through writing. From her cliff top cottage she looks across the D'Entrecasteaux Channel to beautiful and enticing North Bruny Island, the subject of this her third publication.

Pontoon at Alonnah

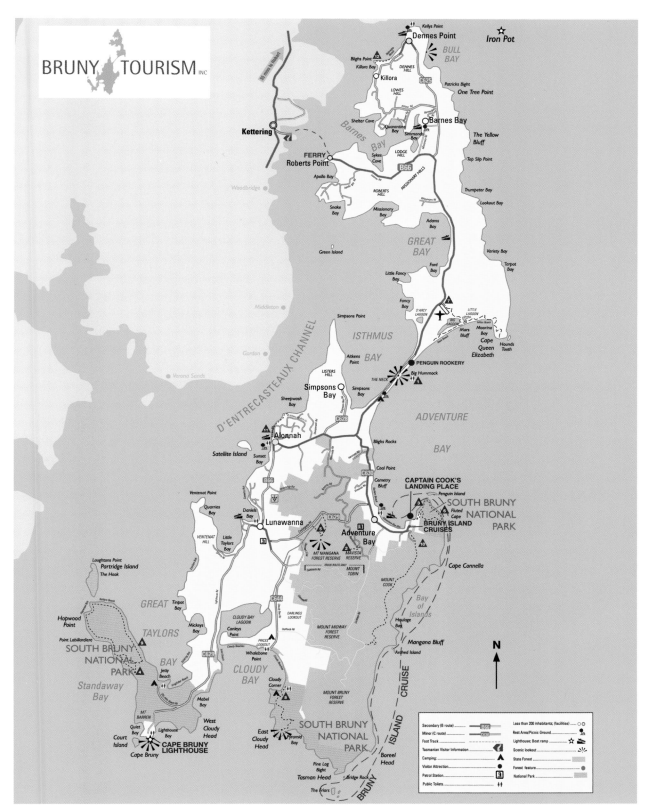

Bruny Island

RECIPE INDEX

ACKNOWLEDGEMENTS

Jill and Richard acknowledge and thank the following people who have assisted us during the production of our book.

Alice Gray

Anna Mead

Anne-Marie Cox

Bev Davis

Bruce and Lynne Michael

Bruny Hotel

Bruny Island history room

Bruny Island Tourism

Chris Paterson

Claire McLaren

David Roberts

Gundars and Lee Simsons

Helen Hussey

Hilary Cane and Bill Erikson

Janice Higgins

Jason Chan

Joanne Rooney

Joan von Bibra

Joe Bennett

John de Rooy

John Moore

Jon Grunseth

Judy Tierney

Kathryn and Graham O'Keefe

Maud de Bohan

Matthew Lillas

Michael Carnes and Bob Lavis

Mick Dudgeon

Mike Annand

Natalie and Grahame Wright

Nick Haddow

Noah and Mia Pennicott

Owen and Dianne Carington-Smith

Oyster Cove Marina

Pauline de Vos

Peter Marmion

Ralph Schwertner

Richard Clarke

Richard and Bernice Woolley

Roger Watson

Ross O'Meara

Sarah and Rick McMahon

Simon Olding (ICC Imagetec)

Susie Bennett

Teresa Derrick

Tony McLaine

Trevor and Sally Adams

Will and Judy Mure

Richard Bennett uses Canon cameras **Canon**